Getting
Serious
ABOUT THE
System

Getting Serious

ABOUT THE

System

A FIELDBOOK
for District and
School Leaders

D'Ette Cowan
Stacey Joyner
Shirley Beckwith

CORWIN
A SAGE Company

CORWIN
A SAGE Company

FOR INFORMATION:

Corwin
A SAGE Company
2455 Teller Road
Thousand Oaks, California 91320
www.corwin.com

SAGE Publications Ltd.
1 Oliver's Yard
55 City Road
London, EC1Y 1SP
United Kingdom

SAGE Publications India Pvt. Ltd.
B 1/I 1 Mohan Cooperative Industrial Area
Mathura Road, New Delhi 110 044
India

SAGE Publications Asia-Pacific Pte. Ltd.
3 Church Street
#10-04 Samsung Hub
Singapore 049483

Acquisitions Editor: Arnis Burvikovs
Associate Editor: Joanna Coelho
Editorial Assistant: Kimberly Greenberg
Production Editor: Amy Schroller
Copy Editor: Brenda Weight
Typesetter: Hurix Systems Pvt. Ltd.
Proofreader: Victoria Reed-Castro
Indexer: Maria Sosnowski
Cover Designer: Scott Van Atta
Permissions Editor: Karen Ehrmann

Printed in the United States of America

A catalog record of this book is available from the Library of Congress.

ISBN 978-1-4522-0511-3

This book is printed on acid-free paper.

SUSTAINABLE FORESTRY INITIATIVE
Certified Chain of Custody
Promoting Sustainable Forestry
www.sfiprogram.org
SFI-01268
SFI label applies to text stock

12 13 14 15 16 10 9 8 7 6 5 4 3 2 1

Contents

Additional materials and resources related to
Getting Serious About the System can be found at
http://www.corwin.com/gettingserious

Preface

How to Use *Getting Serious About the System*

WHY THIS BOOK?

In his foreword to Michael Fullan's 2010 publication, *All Systems Go*, Peter Senge raises a critically important question: "Are we ready to get serious?" Citing America's penchant for quick fixes, silver bullets, and one-size-fits-all solutions to educational problems, Senge states that searching for the one right answer to education's problems may be part of the problem itself. That mentality keeps us "in the box" and disguises the need for overhauling the system itself. True educational change entails much more than addressing only one aspect, or component, of the system, because multiple aspects are integrally related. It also requires increasing the competencies of individuals within the system, as well as their collective capacity, to identify and then address the root cause(s) of their problems.

If we need to get serious about addressing the interrelated components and building the individual and collective capacity of everyone within the system, how is that done, and what is our plan of action? What tools and resources will we need? Where do we begin?

Getting Serious About the System describes a process, grounded in research, for starting and aligning improvement efforts at the district, school, and classroom levels. While the process is intended to be implemented in the local system, it takes into consideration factors at the national, state, and intermediate agency levels. It identifies components of the system that need to be considered as the focus for improvement—standards, curriculum, instruction, assessment, resources, professional staff, policy and governance, and family and community. Its approach also provides a defined, but flexible, process for sustaining improvements by building competencies throughout the system to increase coherence; collect, interpret, and use data; ensure continuous professional learning; build professional relationships; and respond to changing conditions.

What Makes This Book Unique?

Connects Levels of the System

An emerging body of research supports the need to build districts' capacity to help schools improve. While many books have been written about school improvement, *Getting Serious About the System* begins the improvement process by "getting serious" at the district level and then shows how to extend the effort to the school and classroom levels.

Translates Research Into Practice

With increased pressure from federal and state agencies to incorporate research-based strategies into their improvement efforts, district and school leaders may sometimes find themselves struggling to respond to that pressure. This book emphasizes the importance of using research in the improvement effort and goes a step further by providing specific tools, processes, and resources to enable leaders to translate research into practice.

Provides Step-by-Step Guidance

Reform of this nature requires skilled leadership to help create a context for change, develop necessary knowledge and competencies, and establish structures and practices to support and maintain improvement. Workable processes for district and school improvement are described in detail in modules accessible online with the purchase of this book.

Organizes Selected Research on Systemic Improvement

Getting Serious About the System offers educational leaders an extensive bibliography of professional literature mapped to essential components of systemic improvement. As the improvement work progresses at the district, school, and classroom levels, this bibliography will be an important resource for leaders as they investigate research-based strategies to address identified needs.

Provides a "Real-Life" Picture of What the Work Looks Like

Vignettes after each phase of the systemic process help to increase the understanding of each phase by providing leaders with a picture of how the work might play out in typical districts and schools. Descriptions of challenges likely to occur in the process help the reader anticipate issues that may arise and suggest ways for facilitators to respond to them.

How to Use This Book

The materials for *Getting Serious About the System* include this fieldbook, which provides an introduction to systemic improvement and detailed descriptions of each phase of the systemic approach. The fieldbook also provides access to online modules for Phases I, II, and III. (Phases IV and V do not require modules.) Each module contains a scripted facilitator guide, PowerPoint slides, tools, and handouts to help leadership teams carry out the improvement work.

	xx minutes	The amount of time a segment should take
	Handouts x & x	Handouts for the segment
	Whole group	Activity done with the whole group
	Table group	Activity done with the table group
	Partner	Activity done with a partner
	Small groups	Activity done in small groups
	Individual	Activity done individually
	Slides x-x	The slides to be used, at designated points
		Suggested script for the facilitator

Throughout the facilitator guides, icons indicate certain features that will help leaders use the guides successfully. (See chart on next page.)

All members of the district and school leadership teams should have a copy of the fieldbook (and access to the modules) as they work through the systemic improvement process.

A companion book titled *A Teacher's Guide for Getting Serious About the System* (available from Corwin) provides basic information about systemic improvement so that everyone participating in the work (district staff, teachers, school board members, and other stakeholders) has a fundamental understanding of what will be involved and how the work will proceed. It is suggested that this book be distributed as initial decisions about whether or not to engage in the systemic process are being made, and also later as new staff or external partners become involved in the process.

Organization of the Book

Getting Serious About the System begins with an introduction that describes the research base and the development of this approach to systemic improvement. Chapter 1 details each aspect of systemic improvement—the levels of the system, essential components that need to be addressed, and critical competencies that leaders throughout the system need to develop. It also provides a general overview of the five phases of the systemic process and what is accomplished in each.

Each of the following chapters focuses on one of the five phases of the systemic process, beginning with a synopsis of the phase and a brief description of the steps in that phase. A Phase and Competency Matrix serves as a "crosswalk" to identify the primary competencies built during the phase.

Each of the steps within the phases is then further divided into substeps and described in detail, with references to online modules as they are needed. The "Stop and Check" reminder at the end of each step helps ensure that important actions have been completed before moving to the next step. Each phase concludes with a vignette about a fictitious district (Grandville School District) and one of its schools (Delightful Intermediate School). The vignettes describe typical challenges and successes experienced by those leading and implementing the systemic process.

Acknowledgments

This fieldbook is based on and draws heavily from two books on the Working Systemically approach. *Working Systemically to Increase Student Achievement: A Facilitator's Handbook* (2005) was developed by Southwest Educational Development Laboratory (SEDL) and the Charles A. Dana Center at the University of Texas at Austin. The individuals who facilitated the Working Systemically approach in classrooms, schools, and districts across the southwest region contributed invaluable expertise and demonstrated a passion for school improvement throughout its development. A second book, *Working Systemically in Action: A Guide for Facilitators* (2008), was a revision of the 2005 edition and represents the work of many SEDL staff, consultants, and other individuals. We sincerely thank everyone who has shared his or her knowledge and expertise as a part of this effort to increase student achievement.

Contributors to the original *Working Systemically to Increase Student Achievement: A Facilitators' Handbook* were Stella Bell, Janice Bradley, D'Ette Cowan, Vicki Dimock, W. David Hill, Ted Hull, Stacey Joyner, Tom McVey, Ann Neeley, David Rainey, Deborah Reed, Shae Small, William Sommers, Tara Leo Thompson, Ed Tobia, Emma Trevino, Judy Wasaith, and Sebastian Wren.

Graphics were designed by Luis Martinez.

Publisher's Acknowledgments

Corwin would like to thank the following individuals for taking the time to provide their editorial insight and guidance:

Sally Bennett, Curriculum Coordinator
East Poinsett County School District
Lepanto, AR

Freda Hicks, Assistant Principal
Grady Brown Elementary School
Hillsborough, NC

Debbie Langford, Counselor
West Hills Elementary School
Bremerton School District
Bremerton, WA

Marianne Lescher, Principal
Kyrene de la Mariposa School
Gilbert, AZ

Luule Moreno, Independent Educational Consultant
McAllen, TX

Debra Paradowski, Associate Principal
Arrowhead Union High School
Hartland, WI

Diana Pratt, Assistant Principal
Kent Meridian High School
Kent, WA

Cynthia Stone, Director of School Improvement
South San Antonio ISD
San Antonio, TX

Kelly VanLaeken, Principal
Ruben A. Cirillo High School
Macedon, NY

About the Authors

D'Ette Cowan, EdD. Before retiring from SEDL in October 2010, Dr. Cowan led Texas Comprehensive Center efforts to assist state and intermediate agencies in providing high-needs districts and schools with technical assistance that is systemic in nature. In her 12-year career at SEDL, she also assisted low-performing districts and schools throughout a five-state region to improve student learning, and investigated strategies for transforming schools into professional learning communities. Currently, Dr. Cowan serves as a consultant to SEDL on a variety of projects.

As one of the researchers and authors of *Working Systemically in Action: A Guide for Facilitators,* Dr. Cowan has had firsthand experience in helping district and school leaders apply a systemic approach to improve learning outcomes for students. Her study of professional learning communities over her career has included conducting and applying research and presenting findings at conferences and in books and journals. She has authored chapters and articles in *Demystifying Professional Learning Communities: School Leadership at Its Best; SEDL Letter; Journal of School Leadership; Reculturing Schools as Professional Learning Communities;* and *Learning Together, Leading Together.*

Prior to joining SEDL in December 1997, Dr. Cowan served as a junior high school teacher and an elementary school principal. Her continuing research interests include leadership for change, systemic improvement, and professional learning communities.

Stacey Joyner is a Program Associate at SEDL. She participates in efforts to build state education staff capacity to serve districts and schools. She is the former editor of the USDE's Reading First newsletter *The Notebook,* and former editor of the Texas Comprehensive Center's newsletter *Texas Focus.* She is coauthor of SEDL's *Working Systemically in Action: A Guide for Facilitators* that describes a comprehensive process for district and school improvement.

Prior to joining SEDL, Ms. Joyner served as the Reading Coordinator for the Idaho State Department of Education.

She has 11 years of teaching experience. She has served as a reading specialist and teacher trainer for the Clark County School District in Las Vegas, Nevada.

Ms. Joyner holds a BA in Elementary Education from Idaho State University and an MEd in Curriculum and Instruction from the University of Nevada at Las Vegas. She is currently a doctoral student at the University of Texas at Austin.

 **Shirley Beckwith** is a Communications Associate with SEDL's Texas Comprehensive Center (TXCC). She provides editorial review of training materials and resources used in meetings hosted by the TXCC and prepares materials for submission to national evaluators. She also provides and reviews content for the TXCC website. She has been involved in several publications about the Working Systemically approach, including the 2008 *Working Systemically in Action: A Guide for Facilitators,* and helped convert the process into a scripted training manual for school support teams.

Prior to joining SEDL, Ms. Beckwith worked for several years at the University of Texas LBJ School of Public Affairs as the coordinator and researcher for the *Guide to Texas State Agencies.* Ms. Beckwith has a master's degree in library and information science.

Introduction
to Systemic
Improvement

SYSTEMS THINKING

Most of us can recall learning about icebergs at some point in our elementary school science classes. Perhaps the most fascinating fact we remember is that approximately 90% of an iceberg's mass lies below the surface of the water, with only a small portion of the iceberg visible above the surface. Thus, the expression "tip of the iceberg" often refers to how a problem manifests itself at a superficial level. The real causes for the problem lie deep below the surface.

One might ask, "What do icebergs have to do with systemic change?" Senge et al. (2000) use an iceberg analogy to illustrate the necessity of looking below surface events in order to truly understand and then solve school problems. Rather than addressing only the visible aspects of a problem, Senge et al. suggest probing deeper to identify *trends and patterns* in the behavior of an organization (e.g., a school system) to begin revealing the actual source of the problem. However, while identification of these trends and patterns over time is important in analyzing problems, Senge cautions that this information is still inadequate to understand and then address the underlying cause of the problem.

For deeper understanding, Senge and his colleagues suggest delving into *systemic structures* to reveal underlying forces (and interactions among these forces) that contribute to the trends and patterns in organizational behavior. By exploring this deeper level, one can discover fundamental aspects of the system that allow the problem to continue.

Yet, Senge et al. (2000) advocate looking even deeper to consider *mental models* existing within the organization that perpetuate undesirable systemic structures. Such mental models, which are shaped by the values, beliefs, and attitudes of those within the organization, influence both individual and collective views of how the district or school should work. Senge and colleagues propose that systemic thinkers go beyond merely recognizing such models and, instead, honestly question their validity. Challenging these mental models often helps get to the underlying cause of the problem and set the organization on the path toward systemic change.

Systems Thinking in Education

What, then, does systemic thinking have to do with district and school improvement? In 2004, Dennis Sparks, former executive director of the National Staff Development Council (now Learning Forward), noted,

> Every system is specifically designed to produce the results it is getting. The interconnectedness of all parts of the educational enterprise means classrooms, schools, and school districts are tied together in a web of relationships in which decisions and actions in any one part affect the other parts and the system as a whole. (p. 245)

Real change within a local educational system thus requires us to see the connections and "give attention to the interrelationships among multiple aspects of the system so that each is supportive of the others" (Cowan, 2006, p. 597).

Sashkin and Egermeier (1993) describe three traditional approaches to improvement that have shaped school reform efforts during the past half century:

- A "fix the parts" approach that focused only on strengthening key components of the education system, such as curriculum, instruction, and assessment
- A "fix the people" approach that promoted improvement only through staff training and professional development
- A "fix the school" approach that highlighted using only an organizational development perspective to improve individual schools

The authors propose that the lack of success of many educational reform efforts is attributable to exclusive emphasis on only one of these traditional approaches without the others. It is only when these three approaches are integrated and coordinated that significant and sustainable change can be expected.

WORKING SYSTEMICALLY

A Process Grounded in Research

In December 2000, the U.S. Department of Education awarded SEDL (formerly Southwest Educational Development Laboratory) a five-year contract to test a systemic approach designed to improve student achievement in reading or mathematics in low-performing districts and schools. The SEDL team drew upon over two decades of school reform research and theory (e.g., Bossert,

1985; Hallinger & Murphy, 1986; Jenlink, Reigeluth, Carr, & Nelson, 1998; Stringfield, 1995; Teddlie & Stringfield, 1993) to identify the levels, components, and competencies of a systemic approach.

SEDL staff also investigated existing reform models that used a rational process to identify the gaps between effective and low-performing schools (Blum & Landis, 1998; Edmonds, 1979; Lezotte & Jacoby, 1992). However, it soon became apparent that many of these processes addressed only one particular gap, or problem, as it manifested itself at only one level of the system—most often at the building or classroom level. A common strategy used at that time was to find a program to fix one problem, then identify another problem and turn to another program to fix that one.

Additionally, because the underlying causes for gaps and problems were not always explored, schools typically focused on tackling the more apparent "symptoms" of their problems and failed to recognize a fundamental malfunction in the local system. As a result, the underlying problems never got "fixed" and continued to have a negative impact on schools and classrooms. This approach is like seeing water rise in a sinking boat (symptom of a problem) and merely bailing the water out (addressing the symptom) rather than trying to fix the leak (the real problem).

Testing and Refining the Working Systemically Approach

Under its contract with the U.S. Department of Education, SEDL staff worked in 23 districts and 49 schools across its five-state region—Arkansas, Louisiana, New Mexico, Oklahoma, and Texas—to test and refine the Working Systemically approach. Each of the sites in the study included the school district office and at least one school. Some of the sites were rural, some suburban, some urban. All were low performing.

In testing the Working Systemically approach, SEDL staff collected and analyzed data to design, evaluate, and refine specific steps and resources for systemic improvement (Huie, Buttram, Deviney, Murphy, & Ramos, 2004). Student achievement data were collected from partner districts and schools throughout the project. The team used a quasi-experimental design to measure student achievement gains and matched each school in the study to a composite school that represented an aggregate of similar schools in that state.

When viewed across all sites, the achievement gains were mixed, but there were encouraging results. Analyses correlating measures of systemic work and student outcomes across sites showed a statistically significant relationship between increased capacity to work systemically and student achievement in 2003 and 2004.

Results also indicated that activities related to improved alignment of curriculum, instruction, and assessment were most closely related to student achievement. Questions, therefore, began to be raised about the role of the school district in the improvement process and the need to consider the interrelated roles of individuals at multiple levels of the local system as proposed by recent studies (Murphy & Meyers, 2008; Rorrer, Skrla, & Scheurich, 2008; Thornton, Shepperson, & Canavero, 2007).

Overall, three key findings emerged from SEDL's testing of the Working Systemically approach that serve as a foundation for guiding others in the process:

- Districts and schools should stop trying to address every problem with a unique solution and focus their improvement plans on systemic strategies that are small enough to be manageable but large enough to make a difference in student achievement.
- In order to increase the probability of successfully improving student achievement in low-performing systems, the district needs first to concentrate its efforts on aligning curriculum, instruction, and assessment to state standards.
- Leaders at all levels of the system (including teacher leaders) need to support the selected focus for improvement so that the resources of time, personnel, and energy are targeted on that focal point.

THE WORKING SYSTEMICALLY APPROACH

Levels, Components, and Competencies

The Working Systemically approach is a multidimensional process for school improvement that focuses on key *components* of the system that need to be considered in supporting student achievement. It also identifies a core set of *competencies* that leaders in the system need to develop as they address the components. In order to ensure that the improvement is sustained over time, the approach targets multiple *levels* of the system. The goal of the approach is to address the components and competencies at all levels, thereby resulting in systemwide improvement to increase student achievement.

The systemic improvement process described in *Getting Serious About the System,* as well as an earlier SEDL publication, *Working Systemically in Action* (Cowan, Joyner, & Beckwith, 2008), is based on what was learned in documented reports of SEDL's work with schools and districts. The approach includes processes for strengthening informed decision making, effective leadership, supportive school cultures, professional growth, and innovation and continuous improvement while maintaining a focus on student learning (SEDL, 2000, p. 6). This fieldbook, however, provides more detailed information than previous publications on how a district or external facilitator can go about implementing systemic improvement.

What It Takes

The effort required to implement systemic improvement should not be underestimated. Adopting new and more effective research-based practices often requires changing long-established habits and patterns. SEDL's systemic approach addresses the issues (at all levels of the system) that have the most impact on student achievement and increase the competencies of everyone (at all levels of the local system) involved in the improvement work.

As a result, most districts and schools must make some fundamental changes in how they operate. To support these changes, the processes described in this book provide strategies to encourage and nurture effective leadership, as well as a culture that promotes collaboration and networking, continuous learning, and professional respect.

In most cases, district and school leaders should commit to three to five years of work rather than expecting a "quick fix" to improvement. Because this approach is designed to change fundamental aspects of the local system, adequate time and other resources must be allotted to make this a reality. This does not mean, however, that quick wins cannot be attained early in the process. Research indicates the importance of quick wins to build momentum and early support from a critical mass of individuals in an organization (Herman et al., 2008).

Furthermore, the Working Systemically approach requires that the local educational system demonstrate the following:

- A long-term commitment by leaders at the school and district levels to be actively engaged in the improvement process
- An initial focus on ensuring alignment of curriculum, instruction, and assessment to common core or state standards
- A commitment to collecting, interpreting, and using data to develop and monitor the improvement plan
- A sense of ownership and responsibility for improvement by staff members at all levels of the system

Systemic improvement also requires skilled leadership to help create a context for change, develop necessary knowledge and competencies, and establish structures and practices to support and maintain improvement. It is recommended that at least one individual who leads the improvement effort be knowledgeable about research related to organizational change and leadership. This person can help establish critical structures and build leadership knowledge and skills. Another individual should have special knowledge and skills in curriculum and instruction. He or she helps district and school staff identify weaknesses in teaching and learning and guides them toward research-based, content-specific strategies to improve instruction. These two individuals should collaborate throughout all aspects of the work and complement each other to establish an integrated system for sustainable improvement. The dual focus demonstrates the value of teamwork and collaboration in addressing all aspects of the improvement effort.

Summary

This introduction is intended to describe the scope and intensity of a systemic approach to improvement that will lead to increased student achievement.

The approach is not another quick fix that addresses only a single aspect of the educational system. Rather, it provides a process for promoting a culture of continuous inquiry, networking, and collaboration, as well as structures and leadership roles that support and sustain both student and staff learning. Grounded in research, this fieldbook provides online tools and resources designed to assist district and school leaders in achieving this goal.

1

The "Works" of Working Systemically

The Working Systemically approach focuses on three dimensions of the system that must be considered in order to effect deep and lasting improvement: *levels*, *components*, and *competencies*.

Figure 1.1   Working Systemically Dimensions

LEVELS OF THE SYSTEM

A systems approach involves all levels of the educational enterprise (i.e., national, state, intermediate agencies, district, school, and classroom). These levels designate "the who" of the system. Improvement efforts designed to increase student achievement must be coordinated at each of these levels because each level plays a critical part in supporting and sustaining student achievement. When these levels are coordinated and working toward the same goal, they can provide a strong network of support for increased student achievement. Listed in the following paragraphs are the six levels of the system that are integrated throughout the Working Systemically approach.

National Level

The national level is where policy is established for federal education funding, along with guidelines for how those funds are distributed and monitored. In recent years, the national level is where dramatic steps have been taken to establish common core state standards to ensure that students across the nation are college and career ready at the end of high school. The national level also oversees large-scale data collection across the states and provides resources for dissemination of research. This level serves to focus national attention on key educational issues and ensures equal access to education.

State Level

States enact statewide educational policy; allocate funds; and prescribe mandates, guidelines, incentives, and sanctions designed to support and ensure student achievement. Some states also identify their own standards that define what students are supposed to know and be able to do at designated grade levels, as well as oversee assessments of student achievement and statewide accountability systems. Technical assistance for schools in need of improvement is also often provided through statewide efforts.

Intermediate Agency Level

Intermediate agencies (e.g., education service centers, universities) are authorized to implement initiatives assigned by the legislature or education commissioner and to assist districts and schools in operating more efficiently and effectively. Core services provided by this level of the system include training to improve instruction and program implementation, as well as special assistance to low-performing schools. Intermediate agencies also assist districts in complying with state laws and rules and with state or federal special education requirements. This level of the system provides training and assistance to teachers, administrators, members of district boards of education, and members of site-based decision-making committees.

District Level

Local policies are a vital part of improving student achievement. In addition to developing those policies, districts determine how policy is implemented and how personnel and other resources are allocated. In recent years, districts have become increasingly accountable for the learning outcomes of students in the schools within the districts. Boards of education, administrators, and district leadership teams are called on to establish local educational priorities and help maintain the focus on improving student learning. In addition, districts create curricula aligned to common core or state standards that guide instruction and assessment at the school level.

School Level

The school level has long been the focal point for most accountability systems aimed at improving student achievement. This is the level where teachers and administrators collaborate to develop structures and processes to support teaching and learning. A primary responsibility at this level is ensuring alignment of instruction and assessment to the district curriculum. The culture established at the school level determines the extent to which structures, processes, and relationships support student and teacher growth.

Classroom Level

It is at this level where teachers create the conditions in which students can acquire the knowledge and skills prescribed by standards and curriculum documents. It is here that teachers implement instructional strategies and where students and teachers interact directly with the content. Relationships established at this level are extremely critical to the overall culture of the school and can enhance or diminish the context in which students learn.

COMPONENTS OF THE SYSTEM

The components represent "the what" of the system. Eight components in the Working Systemically approach are the aspects of the education system on which schools, districts, and state departments typically focus their work. Processes that support each of the components need to be planned and coordinated with the common intention of meeting student achievement goals.

Standards

Standards define and describe what students are expected to know and be able to do in broad terms at defined intervals of their educational experience. The present effort to establish common core state standards highlights the importance of rigorous expectations to ensure that students are college and career ready to participate in the global community upon high school completion. Whereas most districts and schools use standards as the basis for their curriculum, high-performing schools and districts take time to examine the standards deeply and determine how to include them in a curriculum. Because states are increasingly aligning their assessments to these standards, an excellent starting point for beginning the improvement work is ensuring that district and school staff fully understand what students must know and be able to do to meet each standard.

Curriculum

Curriculum defines more precise district expectations of what students should know and be able to do and ideally provides a scope and sequence for learning, as well as appropriate instructional strategies and resources. A high-quality curriculum is aligned to common core or state standards and provides a road map to ensure coherence across subject areas and grade levels, making it easier for schools and teachers to organize and deliver instruction.

Instruction

Instruction is the "how" of teaching and includes the strategies used to deliver the district's curriculum. Effective teachers select evidence-based instructional strategies and ensure that their instruction addresses the needs and interests of individual students. They continually analyze the impact of their instruction on student achievement through examination of student work and collaborate regularly to enhance their individual and collective capacity to help students achieve expected learning outcomes.

Assessment

Assessment consists of formal and informal procedures that provide teachers, schools, districts, and states a means for measuring student progress toward meeting state standards and goals set by the district and school. A viable assessment system uses multiple sources of data that measure student progress on an ongoing basis. Assessment data can also provide information about the effectiveness of specific improvement initiatives, as well as instructional strategies and resources designed to improve student performance.

Resources

Resources include financial and other assets available to a system that provide qualified and effective staff, instructional materials and equipment, and facilities that support learning. Resources also include the time available for instruction, professional collaboration, and staff learning. In effective systems, decisions about resource allocation are aligned to priority district and school goals and support ongoing improvement efforts.

Professional Staff

Professional staff takes into consideration the recruitment and retention of high-quality personnel across the system. Decisions about the selection, development, and assignment of staff should reflect the needs, focus areas, and priorities of the system. As a primary resource at all levels of the system, the staff's knowledge, skill, and commitment will largely determine the successful outcome of any educational improvement initiative.

Policy and Governance

Policy and governance describe the rules and procedures—conceived at the national, state, and local levels—that are to be followed and how decisions are made to implement those rules and procedures. While policy focuses primarily on written rules and procedures, governance refers to the actions that leaders take to implement the policies and procedures. In some cases, governance is carried out by a group of individuals—the school board, for example. More frequently, it is carried out by formal and informal leaders who have responsibility for implementing policies and demonstrate a sense of urgency for moving their district and schools to higher levels of performance.

Family and Community

Family and community involvement is an essential component in the educational system and can do much to facilitate the improvement work at the district, school, and classroom levels. Systems that actively seek strong family and community partnerships examine structural and psychological barriers that inhibit healthy relationships and seek multiple ways to connect to external entities to develop and reach shared goals. Positive connections among teachers, parents, schools, and the community can help identify and utilize the many available resources that schools can draw upon to support student learning.

COMPETENCIES FOR WORKING SYSTEMICALLY

School improvement approaches commonly focus on one or more of the components of the system described previously. However, without development of special competencies to work on these components, sustainable systemic improvement is not likely to occur. The Working Systemically approach focuses on building these competencies across all levels as the improvement work is conducted. Maintaining a focus on these competencies is an extremely critical aspect of building system capacity to sustain improvement over time.

Creating Coherence

Creating coherence involves taking separate parts of a system and integrating them to achieve desired outcomes (Corallo & McDonald, 2002; Newmann, Smith, Allensworth, & Bryk, 2001). Low-performing districts and schools typically respond to accountability systems and state and federal mandates in a piecemeal fashion. When a new need emerges, a new "fix" (often a new program) is found. This approach creates a fragmented system with little or no coherence among the "fixes."

With many different disconnected and incoherent reform efforts going on at once, people may work hard but become discouraged when they do not achieve desired results. Additionally, teachers and administrators often lack clarity about what the state standards require students to know and be able to do. In such cases, teachers draw almost exclusively from their textbooks and personal preferences for what should be taught and assessed. Teachers are sometimes unaware of research-based instructional strategies that actively engage students in learning. Administrators may have limited knowledge of what they should be looking for in classroom visits, how professional development should be designed, and where they should allocate their limited resources.

SEDL's systemic approach promotes a shared understanding of the extent to which curriculum, instruction, and assessment are aligned to state standards within the local system. It involves district and school leaders actively supporting a coordinated effort in this respect and avoiding competing priorities. Through both actions and words, effective leaders continually reinforce the premise that developing successful students who can meet challenging standards is the system's top priority. Engaging stakeholders at the classroom, school, and district levels in collaborative and purposeful work to improve teaching and learning is essential for creating a coherent instructional focus.

The following questions should guide the work to build this competency in regard to alignment of curriculum, instruction, and assessment to standards—a critical aspect of a coherent system:

- Does the system have a curriculum that is aligned to state standards?
- Does the system ensure that the selection of programs and use of resources are aligned to the curriculum and student needs?
- Does the system have a curriculum scope and sequence that identifies what students should know and be able to do at each grade level?
- Does the system communicate a clear expectation that teachers use a curriculum aligned to state standards to guide their instruction?
- Does the system ensure that content expertise is available and utilized appropriately so that research-based strategies are used in the classroom?

Collecting, Interpreting, and Using Data

Collecting, interpreting, and using data is essential to making sound decisions about improving schools and districts. Identifying trends and patterns in data from multiple sources helps leaders discover underlying factors contributing to core issues and problems that need to be addressed. A deeper understanding of the nature and underlying causes of student achievement challenges in the system enables leaders to make decisions that will lead to long-term solutions.

Many districts and schools typically examine data only in the form of student test results, without exploring underlying causes of low student achievement. As a result, they often act on hunches or beliefs that may or may not accurately represent what actually exists. This competency entails collecting data from multiple sources, arranging the data in formats that help individuals interpret them and draw conclusions, and using information from the data to take appropriate action (Bernhardt, 2004).

SEDL's systemic approach calls for building the capacity of the district and school staff to collect, interpret, and use data effectively. Trends and patterns in student learning data become apparent in longitudinal arrays of data. The achievement levels of various demographic groups of students within the school and district are disaggregated to identify where strengths and weaknesses exist. Perceptual data, collected through surveys and interviews with teachers, administrators, and other stakeholders, are studied to uncover underlying attitudes and beliefs that influence action. School process data are used to determine, for example, how well district and school teams are functioning and whether professional development is affecting attitudes, beliefs, and actions. This information is crucial to effective improvement planning.

The following questions should guide the work to build this competency:

- Does the system have a process and resources for collecting and disaggregating student learning data and organizing them in understandable and useful formats?
- Does the system use multiple types of data (student achievement, demographic, perceptual, and school process) to gain a better understanding of problems and to formulate plans?
- Does the system have processes for turning data into actions that provide timely interventions for students who are not mastering the standards?

Ensuring Continuous Professional Learning

Systems that ensure continuous professional learning provide job-embedded opportunities for all staff to develop their knowledge and skills. Key elements of effective professional learning critical for sustaining improvement include

- relevance to district and school goals, needs, skill levels, and learning preferences of participants;
- a process that is long term and integrated into daily practice; and
- feedback to teachers about their progress in using the knowledge and skills learned (Mid-continent Research for Education and Learning, 2003).

Ensuring continuous professional learning needs to be ongoing, related to teacher and student needs, and embedded in the day-to-day work of planning and delivering instruction (Sparks & Hirsh, 1997). Successful educational systems use multiple forms of data to identify needs of the staff for training and development. In these systems, principals participate actively in professional development sessions and take part in planning, conducting, implementing, and evaluating the effort. Schools that place an importance on professional learning provide adequate time for staff development and follow-up. In these schools, teachers are provided multiple opportunities for networking and receive the ongoing support and materials they need as they implement new instructional strategies.

The Working Systemically approach emphasizes professional learning that includes job-embedded opportunities for all staff to develop the knowledge and skills that are most effective for helping students achieve desired learning outcomes. The approach increases teachers' content expertise and promotes professional conversations about what to teach, how best to teach it, and how to adjust instruction to enable all students to meet the standards.

The following questions should guide the work to build this competency:

- Does the system set clear expectations for improving professional practice at all levels of the local system?
- Does the system ensure that professional learning opportunities are data driven?
- Does the system ensure that professional learning about research-based strategies is provided?
- Does the system provide adequate time for job-embedded professional learning that promotes collaboration and active participation?
- Does the system monitor the implementation and impact of new strategies and practices?

Building Relationships

Building relationships within the system does not happen serendipitously. District and school leaders must be deliberate in creating structures and processes that promote collaboration and collegiality. Ideally, teachers from different grade levels, subject areas, schools, and school districts collaborate and network regularly with one another to share their knowledge, ideas, and strategies. Additionally, school, district, family, and community leaders work together on a common vision for improving schools.

Research demonstrates the importance of building professional relationships based on mutual respect and trust in the improvement process (Bryk & Schneider, 2002). Within a context that supports change and inquiry, individuals throughout the system create a common vision and sense of community as they undertake challenges. Professional conversations about issues related to student achievement, in an environment in which individuals feel free to ask questions and actively listen to others, promote strong and productive relationships in districts and schools. The fundamental purpose of such interactions is to foster a shared understanding of and commitment to improvement efforts.

Low-performing districts and schools often need structures and processes for collaboration and professional conversations. Inadequate attention to building relationships prevents district and school leaders from knowing what teachers need in order to implement changes in instructional practices. Additionally, teachers frequently receive mixed messages about expectations and have limited information about what is being taught or what instructional strategies are being used by other teachers in their own department or grade level.

District and school leadership teams need to provide structures for professional conversations and problem solving around issues central to student learning. The conversations provide insight on the needs of individuals at different levels of the system to accomplish the improvement work.

The following questions should guide the work to build this competency:

- Does the system have multiple structures and processes for individuals at different levels of the local system to have professional conversations?
- Does the system encourage positive interactions among staff members?
- Does the system encourage positive interactions among schools—both vertically and horizontally?
- Does the system encourage positive interactions between the district and the schools?
- Does the system encourage positive interactions between the district/schools and the community?

Responding to Changing Conditions

Educational systems today must adapt to myriad demographic, societal, economic, and political changes. National legislation, state accountability systems, parents, and other stakeholders exert pressure on districts and schools to change. The ability to respond effectively to changing conditions requires identifying and proactively addressing emerging or evolving issues that affect student achievement.

Typical changes that districts and schools confront include leadership transitions, resource allocation, availability of high-quality teachers, shifting demographics, state and local politics, and state and national policy. Districts and schools are better equipped to confront these and other pressures when individuals in the organization are aware of appropriate evidence-based solutions and the organization promotes an atmosphere of continuous learning for adults as well as students.

The Working Systemically approach helps districts and schools shift from a reactive to a proactive stance and helps them make connections between changing conditions and their existing improvement efforts. Regular examination of a broad array of data helps to reveal emerging trends. This can allow staff to anticipate needed resources and explore research-based strategies to make decisions about how best to address the changing conditions.

The following questions should guide the work to build this competency:

- Does the system have processes for anticipating and recognizing changing conditions that affect multiple levels of the local system?
- Does the system promote and support innovations that help teachers and leaders respond to changing conditions?
- Does the system keep the focus on teaching and learning when conditions or circumstances change?
- Does the system seek current and relevant research and best practices to address changing conditions?

THE WORKING SYSTEMICALLY APPROACH IN ACTION

The multidimensional nature of the Working Systemically approach implies a dynamic interaction among its three aspects shown in Figure 1.1 on the opening page of this chapter. This book is written to provide guidance for sustainable improvement within three of the six levels of the educational system—the district, school, and classroom levels. Systemic improvement within these levels requires attention to how each of these levels affects and is affected by other levels. However, this does not mean that the national, state, and intermediate agency levels do not enter the picture. As work is being carried out at the local level, it is necessary to give attention to the national, state, and intermediate agency levels as well. For example, while the local system is often required to comply with requirements and policies at the national and state levels (e.g., national and state content and accountability standards), it can also be supported by these and other levels (e.g., intermediate agency) through funding, access to research-based practices, and technical assistance.

Furthermore, intermediate agencies (e.g., education service centers, universities, social service organizations) are often called upon to provide services and technical assistance. A clear example of this interplay among the levels of the system becomes apparent in the current movement for national standards-based reform. State educational agencies and departments are increasingly called to adopt these national standards and to integrate them into their state accountability systems.

Figure 1.2 The Phases of Working Systemically

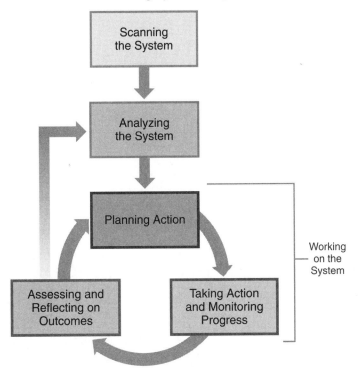

This book describes a process for implementing a systemic approach to improvement at the district, school, and classroom levels (i.e., the local system) and offers guidance and resources to assist leaders at these levels in their efforts. Components and competencies are developed at all levels of the local system through a five-phase process for working in districts and schools to increase student achievement. The five phases of the work provide a framework for transforming an education system. These phases, and their cyclical nature, are illustrated in Figure 1.2.

As stated previously, district and school leaders develop critical competencies as they progress through each phase of the Working Systemically approach. Steps within each phase provide opportunities to focus more intensely on strengthening specific competencies. For example, in Phase II, Analyzing the System, leaders must develop a focus for improvement (create coherence), examine data (collect, interpret, and use data), and work collaboratively with one another (build relationships).

Table 1.1, the Phase and Competency Correlation Matrix, provides a guide to those competencies that receive primary focus during each phase of the Working Systemically approach. However, this does not mean that only those competencies indicated are being developed during any one phase. Because the Working Systemically approach is multifaceted, recursive, and contextual in nature, opportunities will emerge throughout each phase to build the other competencies as well.

Table 1.1   Phase and Competency Correlation Matrix

Key to competencies:

Coherence (Creating coherence)
Data (Collecting, interpreting, and using data)
Professional Learning (Ensuring continuous professional learning)
Relationships (Building relationships)
Change (Responding to changing conditions)

PHASE	Coherence	Data	Professional Learning	Relationships	Change
Phase I: Understanding Systemic Improvement Purpose: Develop an understanding of the systemic improvement process		X		X	
Phase II: Analyzing the System Purpose: Organize leadership teams that understand how the work will affect instructional practice to provide quality learning for all	X	X		X	
Phase III: Planning Action Purpose: Explore research-based strategies for providing quality learning for all and consider how actions can be incorporated into improvement plans; develop or revise improvement plan	X	X	X		X
Phase IV: Taking Action and Monitoring Implementation Purpose: Establish frameworks for meeting regularly, implementing strategies, and monitoring improvement efforts	X	X	X	X	X
Phase V: Assessing and Reflecting on Outcomes Purpose: Determine to what degree the improvement plan is being implemented and monitored; analyze actions in relation to intended outcomes	X	X		X	X

Phase I: Understanding Systemic Improvement

In Phase I, district and school leaders develop an understanding of systemic improvement and how it can be implemented within the system. Leaders begin to develop the system's competencies of building relationships and collecting, interpreting, and using data. This phase of the work consists of four steps:

1. Study the Approach

2. Collect and Analyze Preliminary Data

3. Present the Approach at the School Level

4. Commit to Systemic Improvement

Phase II: Analyzing the System

The purpose of Phase II is to organize district and school leadership teams that identify critical needs in one of the components of the system (discussed earlier). In this phase of the work, the leadership team members envision how the work will have a direct and positive impact on district/school functioning and on instructional practice in the classroom. The competencies of collecting, interpreting, and using data; creating coherence; and building relationships play important parts in this phase, which consists of eight steps:

1. Form the District and School Leadership Teams

2. Begin the Comprehensive Needs Assessment

3. Conduct a Gap Analysis

4. Begin the Process at the School Level

5. Formulate Problem Statements

6. Describe the Ideal State

7. Review District Initiatives

8. Continue the Process at the School Level

Phase III: Planning Action

In Phase III, leaders gain more insight into what research shows to be effective for increasing student achievement and consider how those practices can be incorporated into their improvement effort. Each leadership team also develops a detailed improvement plan that outlines action steps and the support necessary to ensure that the plan will be implemented. The key competencies developed in this phase are collecting, interpreting, and using data; creating coherence; and ensuring continuous professional learning. Planning Action consists of six steps:

1. Investigate Research-Based Practices

2. Explore the Professional Teaching and Learning Cycle (PTLC)

3. Review Progress Made to Date and Existing Plan

4. Develop a District Improvement Plan

5. Formalize and Communicate the District Improvement Plan

6. Develop School Improvement Plans

Phase IV: Taking Action and Monitoring Progress

In Phase IV, leadership teams establish processes for monitoring the implementation and impact of the improvement plans. Leaders and teachers then implement the plans at the district and school levels. Throughout the implementation of the plans, leaders provide the support that is needed in order to maintain momentum and keep the effort on track. In this phase of the work, attention is focused on the competencies of creating coherence; collecting, interpreting, and using data; and ensuring continuous professional learning. Taking Action and Monitoring Progress consists of three steps:

1. Implement and Monitor the Improvement Plans

2. Provide Continuing Leadership for the Improvement Work

3. Address Unique Challenges as They Arise

Phase V: Assessing and Reflecting on Outcomes

In Phase V, members of the leadership teams begin their formal assessment and reflection with a focus on whether and to what degree improvement plans are being implemented with fidelity. They also examine whether the actions taken are resulting in their intended outcomes. Finally, leaders determine at what point in the process their improvement efforts will resume in the following school year. The competencies of collecting, interpreting, and using data and responding to changing conditions are at the forefront of the work in this phase. Assessing and Reflecting on Outcomes consists of three steps:

1. Analyze and Reflect on Evidence of Implementation and Impact

2. Decide on a Focus for Continuing the Improvement Work

3. Recognize Work, Progress, and Accomplishments

Addressing each of the three dimensions of systemic improvement—levels, components, and competencies—may seem daunting at first. However, the following chapters, as well as the online tools and resources, provide needed guidance and support for getting started and sustaining the effort over time.

Additional materials and resources related to
Getting Serious About the System can be found at
http://www.corwin.com/gettingserious

2

Phase I

Understanding Systemic Improvement

Understanding Systemic Improvement is the first of five phases in the process detailed in *Getting Serious About the System*. In this phase, key leaders come to understand what systemic change is and its implications for the local district and schools. Leaders also review preliminary data and ensure that other key staff at the district and school levels are committed to changes that the work may require. Two competencies are the focus during this phase: building relationships and collecting, interpreting, and using data (see Figure 2.1, p.22). The phase consists of four steps:

Step 1. Study the Approach. Key leaders begin developing an understanding of systemic improvement and its implications for district and school staff.

Step 2. Collect and Analyze Preliminary Data. Leaders collect and review preliminary data and decide which schools will likely be the first to participate in the systemic improvement process.

Step 3. Present the Approach at the School Level. Leaders introduce the new approach to the principal and staff of each selected school.

Step 4. Commit to Systemic Improvement. Leaders debrief the school meetings, review the implications and commitments of a systemic approach to improvement, and make a decision about moving forward.

Figure 2.1 Competencies Developed in Phase I

PHASE	Competencies				
	Coherence	Data	Professional Learning	Relationships	Change
Phase I: Understanding Systemic Improvement Purpose: Develop an understanding of the systemic improvement process		X		X	

The steps in this first phase of the work help district and school leaders embark on systemic improvement by using data to guide decision making and promoting collaborative processes. The working relationships among the district and school leaders and with education leaders external to the local educational system are critical because systemic change requires a high level of collaboration, communication, and trust.

STEP 1. STUDY THE APPROACH

1.1 Study the Systemic Approach to Improvement With Key Leaders

Prior to undertaking systemic improvement, key district leaders, particularly the superintendent, need to develop a solid understanding of the systemic approach and the demands for effective leadership at all levels of the local system. The superintendent convenes a meeting of key leaders to accomplish this. Ideally, the participants at the meeting should include representation from instructional, administrative, and curricular areas of the system. It is also advisable to include family and community representatives in this initial meeting as well as successive ones. Research has shown that parent and community involvement is one of the "essential supports" necessary for school reform (Bryk, Sebring, Allensworth, Luppescu, & Easton, 2010).

During this first meeting, participants use the **Overview Module,** which can be found in the Phase I section of the online materials that accompany this book. The materials in this module are designed to be used as a foundation for understanding what the improvement effort will entail. The **Overview Module** contains a Facilitator's Guide that gives detailed instructions on how to introduce and discuss the systemic improvement process. The module also contains a PowerPoint presentation and handouts that include an introduction to systemic improvement, graphic representations of key aspects of the systemic approach, a rubric to determine system capacity, some guiding questions for conversations regarding the approach, and a bibliography. The publications listed in the bibliography provide information and research on systemic improvement and the infrastructure and culture required for its successful implementation.

1.2 Discuss Implications of Systemic Improvement for the District

Leaders must understand the implications of a systemic approach for the local district and schools, including the scope of the work at each of these levels, roles that individuals will perform, and the benefits for staff and students. These discussions require open and honest consideration of the readiness and willingness of leaders and other staff to commit to the work.

It may be useful to refer to the following expectations and commitments for systemic improvement to inform this discussion.

Stable Leadership. Systemic improvement requires a long-term process; therefore, stable leadership is vital to its success. If the superintendent or other key leaders are planning to retire or leave the district, the decision on whether or not to undertake the improvement effort should be delayed until after the transition so that the new leaders can be involved in the decision.

Authentic Involvement of Leaders. District and school leaders will need to be actively involved in the improvement process. They cannot stand on the sidelines or appoint someone else to provide leadership while they attend to routine matters. The active involvement of formal leaders, in particular, provides a powerful message about the urgency and importance of the improvement work. At the same time, formal leaders should always be attuned to ways to build leadership capacity throughout the levels of the system.

Systemwide Participation in Data Collection. Systemic improvement requires that leaders make thoughtful decisions based on multiple forms of data. Leaders must frequently engage staff members in data collection and analysis to monitor the extent to which improvement efforts are being implemented as intended, and whether these effort are having the desired impact.

Systemwide Use of Research. Staff at all levels of the system will need to study and use current research on strategies for improvement to inform their decisions. In many cases, this will mean that long-standing practices and ways of interacting that have had little or no effect on student learning will need to be replaced with more effective ones.

(Continued)

(Continued)

Commitment to a Long-Term Improvement Effort. Implementing a complex approach that involves substantive organizational and individual change at multiple levels of a system requires a long-term commitment. During this time, district and school leaders continually develop the competencies needed to sustain improvement.

Commitment to a Systemic Approach and Goals. The improvement work requires involvement from, and a focus on, multiple levels and aspects of the system. If district and school leaders are focused on improving only a single element of the system (e.g., a single grade level, family and community involvement, or professional learning), then the improvement work ceases to be systemic in nature. In this case, another approach may be better suited to help leaders accomplish these goals.

Commitment to Supporting the Participation and Time of Teachers and Leaders. Systemic improvement requires the formation of a district leadership team to direct and monitor the improvement work. Similarly, key leaders at the school level will need to be organized and involved in implementing the improvement plan. Within the schools, teams of teachers must have time and support for collaborating on ways to improve instruction, as well as access to high-quality professional development.

Commitment to Focused, Ongoing, Job-Embedded Professional Learning for Leaders and Staff. Professional learning on the part of the adults in a system must precede increased learning on the part of students. Districts and schools characterized as learning organizations promote systemwide and school-based opportunities to integrate collaborative professional learning strategies into all their work. They also provide ongoing support and follow-up to ensure application of their learning in order to improve learning outcomes for students.

Commitment to Making the Improvement Work a Priority. The active participation and support of leaders at the district and school levels (including teacher leaders) is necessary for this effort to be effective. The fact that this work is and continues to be a priority is a key message that needs to be communicated by leaders throughout the duration of the process.

Stop and Check

Before taking the next step, make sure the following events have occurred:

✓ The key leaders have studied the systemic approach to improvement and its demands for strong leadership.
✓ Key leaders have discussed implications for systemic improvement in the local system.

STEP 2. COLLECT AND ANALYZE PRELIMINARY DATA

2.1 Collect and Array Preliminary Data

The primary purpose of collecting initial data at this point is to determine whether the district leaders are ready and willing to enter into a long-term systemic improvement process. This does not mean that everyone in the local system is committed or that the district has the current capacity to make necessary changes. It does mean, however, that key district leaders are willing to explore a commitment to making substantive changes and providing necessary resources.

Data collected at this early stage are preliminary and exploratory in nature, but they provide indicators of the potential success of the undertaking. When multiple sources of data are examined, district and school leaders develop a deeper understanding of factors that are influencing student learning. Bernhardt (2009) presents four categories of data—student learning, perceptions, demographics, and school processes—and stresses the importance of using multiple categories in assessing a school system. Holcomb (2008) recommends that similar data be examined at multiple levels of the system: student performance, stakeholder perceptions, and organizational culture.

An initial assessment of the district and schools under consideration for the systemic improvement work can be especially helpful at this early stage. The Rubric for Determining System Capacity in the **Overview Module** can provide perceptual data about the structure and functioning of the system. Data from this tool could also reveal whether staff members are willing or resistant to committing to the approach, as well as whether they have the capacity to participate in it. These data may be used in a later phase when leaders determine a focus for the improvement work.

In order to be truly systemic, the improvement work should involve all schools in the district. However, it will likely not be feasible to implement it at all schools in the beginning. The data collected during this step will help leaders decide which schools to include in the initial work.

Essential in this initial period of data collection are student achievement data. District and school data from the previous three years should be collected and disaggregated by school, grade, and subpopulations. Arraying data in simple graphic representations will help district and school leaders understand and analyze them. Longitudinal arrays will reveal trends and patterns that indicate where the greatest areas of need exist, particularly content areas. The Sample Graphs of Student Data (Figure 2.2) provides bar graph examples of fifth-grade reading data, displayed by performance level and content standards, over a three-year period. It also shows a single year of reading data, displayed by content standards and disaggregated by student subgroups. This example can be used as a model in creating a data display for the district and schools.

2.2 Analyze Preliminary Data

The leaders should collaboratively analyze the collected data to guide their decision about the schools to be selected initially for systemic improvement.

Figure 2.2 Sample Graphs of Student Data

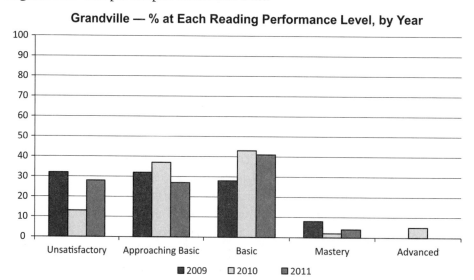

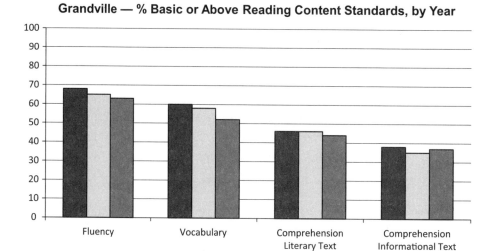

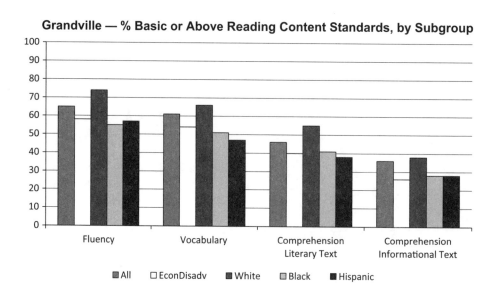

They should also identify initiatives already underway within the district and individual schools. The leaders will need to determine whether the systemic approach would strengthen and complement existing improvement efforts or whether it would conflict with them. The discussion at this time may also indicate the extent to which specific district and school leaders are willing to commit to systemic improvement.

When selecting initial schools for participation, leaders should take several factors into consideration:

- **Schools failing to meet national and/or state standards.** The systemic approach is specifically designed to improve student achievement in schools that are low performing. However, the approach can also assist schools that are already meeting or exceeding standards as they work toward continuous improvement.

- **Schools that are linked.** If district leaders select schools that are linked (e.g., represent a feeder pattern), they will be in a position to work more systemically. This allows them to address important factors—such as a K–12 scope and sequence for targeted content areas—more coherently.

- **Managing change.** District leaders may decide to forgo selecting a school facing other significant changes (e.g., the current principal is leaving, the school will be consolidated into another school) until the situation has stabilized and any incoming leadership has an opportunity to decide whether to participate in the process.

- **Willing participation of school leaders.** Initial resistance to major improvement work is not uncommon and may indicate a need for additional conversations before school leaders agree to participate in systemic improvement.

Once the preliminary decision about the selection of schools is made, the leaders make plans to meet with principals of these recommended schools to discuss whether or not they are willing to participate.

Stop and Check

Before taking the next step, make sure the following events have occurred:

- ✓ The key leaders have reviewed student achievement and other data to inform the selection of initial schools for implementing the approach.
- ✓ The key leaders have recommended schools for the initial improvement work.

STEP 3. PRESENT THE APPROACH AT THE SCHOOL LEVEL

3.1 Meet With Principals of Recommended Schools

Once the preliminary data are analyzed, the superintendent invites principals of schools under consideration to join the conversation about the systemic improvement effort. The superintendent and other district leaders use materials from the **Overview Module**, introduced in Step 1, to provide background information about the approach to school leaders. They also review the student achievement data that helped inform their decision on school selection. The principals need to understand why their schools are being considered and confirm the content areas and subgroups of students that show the greatest need for improvement as indicated by the student achievement data. During this meeting, the superintendent ensures that principals understand the expectations and commitments (see Step 1.2) necessary for the proposed systemic improvement effort. Together, they develop a plan for presenting the data to the staff at each school and describing why each school was recommended as a possible participant in the process.

3.2 Convene a Meeting of All Professional Staff at Each of the Recommended Schools

At each recommended school, the principal and district leaders convene a meeting to inform school-level staff about the systemic improvement effort that is being considered by the district. They distribute the companion book, *A Teacher's Guide to Getting Serious About the System,* to all school staff to help them gain an initial understanding of what will be involved in the systemic improvement work.

The school meeting provides an opportunity to explain the selection of recommended schools and to collect additional data that will provide insight into the school's readiness to engage in the improvement work. In addition to reviewing the systemic improvement process, the principal leads four activities in the meeting:

- **Present the school-level data.** The principal presents the achievement data collected and analyzed by district leaders and encourages school staff members to discuss what they see as the most important information in the data.
- **Review expectations and commitments.** The principal gives an overview of the expectations and commitments for systemic improvement work (from Step 1.2).
- **Respond to questions and concerns from school staff.** The principal and district leaders answer questions from the school staff about how the systemic improvement effort is likely to affect them personally. They should address these questions as openly and honestly as possible.

- **Conduct the circle and squares activity.** The template for the Circles and Squares activity is provided in the **Overview Module** as a means to examine questions and concerns individual staff members may have about the systemic approach but were hesitant to express openly in a discussion. Respondents write what "squares" with their thinking about systemic improvement on the square shape, and what is still "circling" in their heads on the circle shape.

Stop and Check

Before taking the next step, make sure the following events have occurred:

✓ The leaders have met with principals from recommended schools to discuss expectations and commitments needed for the systemic improvement work.

✓ The principal and district leaders have conducted a meeting with school-level staff to review student achievement data, distribute a resource that explains the systemic approach for improvement, discuss expectations and commitments, and respond to questions and concerns.

STEP 4. COMMIT TO SYSTEMIC IMPROVEMENT

4.1 Debrief the School-Level Meetings

The superintendent, other district leaders, and principals then debrief the school-level meetings to decide whether or not to implement the systemic improvement process. The comments from the Circles and Squares activity should be reviewed and discussed. The verbal and written questions and concerns expressed at the school meetings will provide an indication of the schools' readiness and commitment to systemic improvement.

4.2 Decide Whether to Commit to Systemic Improvement

The superintendent further explains the nature of the work and specific commitments involved in implementing the systemic approach. Other stakeholders in the local system should be informed of the approach and given an opportunity to express their opinion and concerns. The following points must be emphasized before reaching a decision on whether or not to agree to the systemic improvement effort:

TIP: To build support and commitment throughout the local system, it is recommended that additional district leaders, principals, school board members, parents, and community members be involved in this decision.

- The district's commitment to systemic improvement
- The schools targeted for initial improvement efforts
- The role of all stakeholders in the systemic improvement process

Stop and Check

Before taking the next step, make sure the following events have occurred:

✓ The leaders have debriefed the school-level meetings.
✓ The leaders have provided an opportunity for other stakeholders to express their opinion and concerns about the systemic approach.
✓ The leaders have decided whether to commit to systemic improvement.

Vignette

PHASE I AT THE GRANDVILLE SCHOOL DISTRICT AND DELIGHTFUL INTERMEDIATE SCHOOL

Grandville School District serves approximately 6,500 children in an agriculture-based community that is about 60 miles from a large city. The district has one high school (Grades 9–12), one middle school (Grades 7 and 8), two intermediate schools (Grades 4–6), and four elementary schools (preK–3). The district demographics reflect 40% Hispanic, 12% African American, and 48% White students.

Avis Dunbar, the district superintendent, has been with the district for three years. Dr. Dunbar is feeling pressure from the school board and the community because student achievement has been falling in some schools for the past two years. She recently attended a state education conference where she learned about a systemic approach for improving student achievement. The district's past efforts at improvement have been fragmented, lacked coherence, and failed to bring about the desired results, so she is looking for a process that is research based and requires some sweeping changes throughout the district.

Study the Approach and Discuss Implications of Systemic Improvement for the District

Dr. Dunbar has learned that before she enters any large-scale improvement effort, she needs to have support from the central office staff and principals. In May, she convenes a meeting of key central office staff and principals to discuss the implications of systemic improvement for the district. They read the description of systemic improvement provided in the **Overview Module** *and scan some of the journal articles that support a systemic approach. They begin to recognize that engaging in this approach requires commitment and sustained efforts to improve; however, they remain open to this being a possible way for lasting improvement*

Collect and Analyze Preliminary Data

In order to determine where to begin, Dr. Dunbar leads the key leaders in an examination of student performance data at the district and school levels for the current year and the two previous years. Based on these data, they determine that three of the schools that need improvement—two intermediate schools and one elementary school—might be good candidates to participate in systemic improvement. After this initial examination, they decide to present the approach to the principals of these schools.

Dr. Dunbar and the key leaders meet with the principals from the selected schools. Mark Martinez, the principal at Delightful Intermediate School, is among the most enthusiastic principals in the district. He is beginning his third year at the school and seems to have a good relationship with teachers and parents at Delightful. The energy and enthusiasm that Mr. Martinez brings to his school reinforces Dr. Dunbar's decision to encourage Delightful to be one of the schools in the systemic improvement effort.

After the meetings with the principals, the leaders discuss the fact that the other intermediate school principal is planning to retire at the end of the next school year. This raises concern about the sustainability of the improvement work at this school. As a result of this discussion, Dr. Dunbar and the key leaders decide to include only Delightful Intermediate School and one of its feeder school—Fairview Elementary—in the initial systemic improvement process.

Present the Approach at the School Level

Dr. Dunbar and the principals of Delightful and Fairview Schools then convene separate meetings with all professional staff at each school. Dr. Dunbar explains the systemic process and what it requires on the part of all professional staff. Mr. Martinez then distributes copies of A Teacher's Guide to Getting Serious About the System and asks teachers to read it before the next faculty meeting. He particularly emphasizes the need for teachers to examine student performance data, collaborate regularly, and explore new instructional strategies. Teachers express concern about changes the systemic process would require. Dr. Dunbar and Mr. Martinez take time to listen to these concerns and to answer questions to help alleviate teachers' apprehensions.

Commit to Systemic Improvement

Most of the specific concerns expressed by the Delightful staff center on the time commitment that any new initiatives will require from teachers who already have busy schedules. Dr. Dunbar and Mr. Martinez admit that teachers will likely be called on to adjust the way they work; however, they remind the staff that changes are necessary in order to ensure the success of Delightful's students. After responding to the concerns about what the work will entail, the staff at Delightful commit to the systemic improvement process. Later, the staff at Fairview also commit to the process.

Additional materials and resources related to
Getting Serious About the System can be found at
http://www.corwin.com/gettingserious

3

Phase II

Analyzing the System

Analyzing the System is the second of five phases in the systemic improvement process. In Phase I, Understanding Systemic Improvement, district leaders used data to make an informed decision on whether or not to commit to long-term systemic improvement. If the leaders, at the end of this first phase, decided to continue with the approach's implementation, they designated the first schools that would participate in the improvement effort and clearly outlined the expectations of those involved.

The purpose of Phase II, Analyzing the System, is to establish membership of district and school leadership teams and identify systemic issues—through a comprehensive needs assessment—that are hindering student achievement. In this phase, the district and school leaders increase their understanding of how the work will directly affect the system as a whole, including instructional practice in the classroom. Analyzing the System consists of eight steps:

Step 1. Form the District and School Leadership Teams. The district and school leaders formally identify who will serve on the leadership teams, convene meetings of the teams, and begin preparing the teams for the work ahead.

Step 2. Begin the Comprehensive Needs Assessment. The district leadership team collects relevant data through the System Alignment Survey, interviews and focus groups, and other sources. These data, in addition to data collected in Phase I, are then organized into a format that will help the team understand the current status of factors affecting student learning.

Step 3. Conduct a Gap Analysis. The district leadership team members examine their own predictions and assumptions about the data to be examined, and then conduct a gap analysis using a System Examination Tool (Handout 1 in the **Gap Analysis Module**). During this process, the team examines the linkage between alignment and student achievement and determines how effectively the local system's curriculum, instruction, and assessment are aligned to the common core or state standards. The team also considers whether there are adequate resources to support alignment and examines the other three components of systemic improvement: professional staff, policy and governance, and family and community. This process helps leaders identify where they should focus their initial improvement efforts.

Step 4. Begin the Process at the School Level. The school representatives to the district leadership team return to their respective schools at this point and duplicate Steps 2 and 3.

Step 5. Formulate Problem Statements. The district leadership team participates in a process to formulate problem statements that summarize major challenges faced by the district.

Step 6. Describe the Ideal State. After a review of research and best practices, the team transforms their problem statements into a description of the ideal state, which articulates what the district, as a system, will be like once the identified problems are solved.

Step 7. Review System Initiatives. After developing the problem statements and using them as a basis for describing the ideal state, the district leadership team reviews and maps out initiatives that are in place within the district and determines which ones will support attainment of the ideal state. Team members refocus on the big picture of systemic improvement and plan next steps.

Step 8. Continue the Process at the School Level. Using input from the district team, the school leadership teams duplicate Steps 5, 6, and 7. In Phase III, the problems statements and ideal state will be used in developing the school improvement plan.

As they follow the steps in Phase II, team members examine their system in more depth and focus their attention on the work ahead. In the often-chaotic environment of a school system struggling to improve, leaders have an opportunity to reflect on previous efforts to juggle multiple priorities that frequently result from expectations of federal and state requirements, parents and community members, staff members, and the students themselves.

Analyzing the System helps district and school leaders begin to take focused, deliberate steps toward specific outcomes. They organize leadership teams with representation from multiple levels to look at the system holistically and set priorities that will focus the improvement work.

Figure 3.1 Competencies Developed in Phase II

PHASE	Competencies				
	Coherence	*Data*	*Professional Learning*	*Relationships*	*Change*
Phase II: Analyzing the System Purpose: Organize leadership teams that understand how the work will impact instructional practice to provide quality learning for all	X	X		X	

STEP 1. FORM THE DISTRICT AND SCHOOL LEADERSHIP TEAMS

1.1 Select Members of the District Leadership Team

TIP: The goal is to select a number of participants large enough to represent the different perspectives but small enough to function effectively. A district leadership team typically functions best when it has between 10 and 16 members.

Having committed to systemic improvement, the first order of business for the superintendent and key leaders is to select members of the district leadership team. This team will coordinate the improvement effort at the district level. The **Team Membership Module** (in the Phase II resources available online) can be used to help leaders identify who should serve on the leadership team. A critical consideration in forming a high-quality district leadership team is its composition and size. Individuals may need to be added to the initial group of team members to ensure that the various levels, roles, and perspectives in the system are represented.

Key functions of the district leadership team include the following:

- Establishing and maintaining the focus for the improvement effort
- Creating and regularly updating the district improvement plan
- Monitoring implementation of the district improvement plan throughout the school year
- Ensuring that necessary support and resources are provided so that staff members can implement the plan effectively
- Ensuring that the improvement effort is—and remains—a system priority
- Assessing outcomes of the work and adjusting the plan accordingly

Three categories (essential, highly recommended, and added value) discussed in the Team Membership Module, can be used to help guide selection of team members. The district leaders can review these categories and select members based on the local context and the analysis of preliminary data from Phase I. In addition to these team member categories, those making the selection should consider the following roles:

- **Informal leaders.** District leaders need to look beyond formal positions or titles and consider individuals who are informal leaders and whose input and support would be an asset to the team. Often these individuals bring viewpoints to the planning process that help tailor a plan for a particular system. Additionally, informal leaders to whom district- and school-level staff turn for information and guidance can help emphasize the importance of the improvement effort, communicate district team deliberations, and build support among staff members throughout the system.

- **Leaders from schools in the same feeder pattern.** The district improvement plan places a priority on aligning the curriculum, instruction, and assessment to common core or state standards. This often means creating or revising the district curriculum and including an instructional scope and sequence for each grade level in the target schools. The results may have substantial implications for instructional planning at those schools. Principals in the feeder pattern should be involved in shaping the district plan to ensure that student progress from one grade level to the next is as smooth and efficient as possible.

- **Representatives from other schools.** It is recommended that principals and leaders from schools other than those directly targeted for the initial work also serve on the district leadership team. Their involvement helps to prepare them for active participation in the improvement process in the future.

- **Individuals with specialized knowledge or experience.** The district leaders identify individuals in the system who have expertise in content areas or experience with special populations of students. They should also consider individuals who are familiar with existing initiatives in the district. These members would help ensure that the district improvement plan does not overlook any student populations and takes into consideration existing improvement efforts. The addition of a person who has skills in data collection and analysis could assist with formatting data in order to help the whole team make informed decisions.

- **Other stakeholders, such as parents, community members, and board members.** These individuals can often provide important perspectives existing outside the system. Effective family and community engagement is an important aspect of systemic improvement and can result in improved student achievement, as well as greater communitywide support for districts and schools. In addition to their official capacity as policymakers, school board members are often in a position to communicate to the community at large and build public support for major improvement initiatives. Involving representation from these constituencies helps promote shared responsibility for student learning.

Small districts that do not have adequate numbers of leaders with the necessary knowledge and skills to fill these roles may choose to invite staff from external assistance providers, such as universities or educational service centers, to serve on the leadership team. A recurring function of the district leadership team will be to examine periodically the composition of the team in relation to the specific focus of the improvement work and adjust it accordingly. Team members should reflect on whether the district team, as composed, represents areas of currently needed expertise and influence.

1.2 Convene a Meeting of the District Leadership Team and Orient Team Members to Their Roles

Once the members of the district leadership team have been identified and their participation confirmed, they meet to discuss what it means to work systemically. They also establish the purpose of the team and how it will function. The leadership team should repeat the process conducted by the key leaders in Phase I, Step 1.1, using the **Overview Module.**

Even though some members of the team may have participated in this process during Phase I, it is beneficial to repeat it. The module will give all team members an understanding of what is involved in the improvement work and what their roles will be. There is much information to assimilate, and further discussion can lead to a more thorough understanding of the systemic process.

The team can establish guidelines through the following activities:

1. Identifying norms for working together. Norms provide guidelines for how the team members will interact, make decisions, and conduct business. They are an important aspect in establishing a culture of collaboration and continuous professional learning, as well as ensuring that meetings are productive and emotionally safe. It may be helpful to revisit the norms at the beginning of each meeting, so that they become an integral part of the meeting process.

The team may want to generate an original list of norms. As an alternative, they can begin with a list of possible norms, similar to those listed below, and revise them as they see fit. Arriving at a consensus on the norms will serve to strengthen professional relationships among team members. Some of the following norms are intentionally broad to cover a variety of team member behaviors and can be used to begin the conversation about how the team will work together:

- Team members will arrive on time.
- Everyone is expected to come prepared and to participate.
- People and their ideas are respected.
- Blaming will get the team nowhere.
- The team should keep the focus on the "main thing" (student achievement).

The team should spend time discussing concrete behaviors that would or would not demonstrate adherence to the norms. For example, by refraining from side conversations while someone "has the floor," the team shows respect for people and their ideas. Additionally, by debriefing previously held professional development—with the intent to improve and build on such experiences rather than criticize them—they practice avoiding blame. Likewise, by making decisions that are intended to increase student achievement but require significant instructional changes on the part of teachers, the team exemplifies keeping the focus on the "main thing."

2. Establishing the purpose and organization of the team. The members of the leadership team serve as liaisons to different groups within the system. Therefore, it is important that they can articulate the purpose of the team and how it will affect the district (or school). The **Team Functions Module** leads the members through a process that helps them establish the team's purpose, members' roles, norms, communication and decision-making guidelines, and other important elements that can help the team function efficiently and effectively.

Knowing the procedures for meetings (e.g., beginning and ending on time, preparing and distributing the agenda in advance, and disseminating meeting notes) is important for successful team functioning. Members need to determine how often they will meet, how long they are expected to serve on the team, and other meeting parameters. Establishing a clear understanding of these issues will help orient members to their individual and collective roles and prepare them to work together as a team.

Before adjourning the initial meeting, team members should schedule additional meetings for the remainder of the school year. The activities in this meeting are important in preparing the team for a crucial step in this phase— conducting a gap analysis.

1.3 Form School Leadership Teams

The school representatives on the district leadership team return to their respective schools at this point and establish school leadership teams. These teams will coordinate the improvement efforts at the school level. The specific configuration of each team depends on the context of the school and its needs. The team configuration may change as the work develops. However, the team should be made up of both formal and informal leaders, including representatives from each grade level or department and other individuals with expertise in specific areas of need as reflected in student achievement and other data.

The **Team Membership Module** can be used again to help school leaders understand the role of their leadership team in the improvement work and identify who should serve on their teams. The module has been designed to work with either the district or school leadership team.

As with the district team, a critical consideration in forming a high-quality school leadership team is its composition and size. The initial team may need to be revised as work progresses to ensure that the various levels, roles, and perspectives in the school are represented.

Key functions of the school leadership team are similar to those at the district:

- Establishing and maintaining the focus for the school's improvement effort
- Creating and regularly updating the school improvement plan

- Monitoring implementation of the improvement plan throughout the school year
- Ensuring that necessary support and resources are provided so that staff members can implement the plan effectively
- Ensuring that the improvement effort is—and remains—a school priority
- Assessing outcomes of the work and adjusting plans accordingly

The same three categories used for the district team (essential, highly recommended, and added value) can also be used to help guide selection of the school team members. Leaders can review these categories and select members based on the local context. In addition to these team member categories, those making the selection should consider the following roles:

- **Informal leaders.** School leaders need to look beyond formal positions or titles and consider individuals who are informal leaders and whose input and support would be an asset to the team. Often these individuals bring viewpoints to the planning process that help tailor a plan for a particular school. Additionally, informal leaders to whom school-level staff turn for information or guidance can help emphasize the importance of the improvement effort, communicate leadership team deliberations, and build support among staff members throughout the school.

- **Individuals with specialized knowledge or experience.** The school leaders identify individuals in the system who have expertise in content areas or experience with special populations of students. They should also consider individuals who are familiar with existing initiatives in the school. These members would help ensure that the improvement plan does not overlook any student populations and takes into consideration existing improvement efforts. The addition of a person who has skills in data collection and analysis could help with formatting data in order to help the whole team make informed decisions.

- **Other stakeholders, such as parents and community members.** These individuals can often provide important perspectives existing outside the school. Effective family and community engagement is an important aspect of systemic improvement and can result in improved student achievement, as well as greater communitywide support for the school. Involving representation from these constituencies helps promote shared responsibility for student learning.

Small schools that do not have adequate numbers of leaders with the necessary knowledge and skills to fill these roles may choose to invite staff from the district or external assistance providers, such as universities or educational service centers, to serve on the leadership team. Each school leadership team convenes an initial meeting of the team and duplicates Step 1.2 at the school level. This includes using the **Overview Module** to give team members an understanding of what is involved in systemic improvement and what their roles will be. Then team members establish norms and use the **Team Functions Module** to establish the purpose and organization of their team, just as the district leadership team did.

A recurring function of the school leadership team will be to examine periodically the composition of the team in relation to the specific focus of the improvement work and adjust it accordingly. Team members should reflect on whether the school team, as composed, represents areas of currently needed expertise and influence.

Stop and Check

Before taking the next step, make sure the following events have occurred:

✓ The superintendent and district/school leaders have selected individuals to serve on the leadership teams, based on their positions, job responsibilities, and perspectives relative to the identified needs.
✓ The leadership teams have convened their first official meeting and established norms for working together.
✓ Members of the leadership teams are demonstrating an emerging understanding of systemic improvement and commitment to their roles in implementing this improvement effort.
✓ Dates and times have been set for additional team meetings in order to complete the steps in this and the next phases of the work.

Figure 3.2 Systemic Planning Process

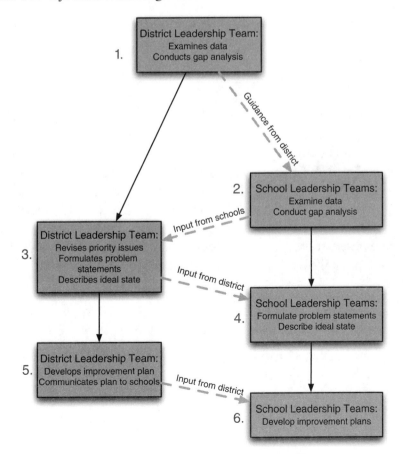

STEP 2. BEGIN THE COMPREHENSIVE NEEDS ASSESSMENT

A critical step in systemic improvement is conducting a comprehensive needs assessment (CNA). The CNA reveals both strengths and challenges in various areas of the district or school. It is a process that should be repeated at least annually to determine where progress is being made and to highlight areas that still need to be addressed. The district leadership team begins the process and then guides the school leadership teams through the steps up to and including the gap analysis. The district and school teams continue the systemic planning process, providing input to one another at various stages.

The CNA is built on data from a variety of sources. Before beginning the assessment, the leadership team should use the **Data Module** to explore types of data that can be collected and analyzed to create a profile of the district/ school. The picture that emerges from the data analysis is then used to guide the systemic improvement effort.

2.1 Examine a Variety of Data Sources

In most schools and districts, when someone mentions data, the first thing that comes to mind is student achievement data. Although these data must be examined, they are not the only type of data to consider. As discussed in the **Data Module,** Bernhardt (2009) describes four categories, or measures, of data that are important to consider: demographics, student learning, school processes, and perceptions. Demographic data can describe the composition of the local system and can be collected through enrollment and attendance records, dropout rates, ethnicity and gender characteristics, and grade-level statistics. Student-learning data provide information about student performance on different assessment measures and can be collected through norm- and criterion-referenced tests, teacher observations, and authentic assessments of student knowledge and skills. School-processes data offer information about educational programs, instruction and assessment strategies, and other classroom practices and can be collected through an analysis of processes and programs being implemented and the results they are producing. Finally, perceptual data can provide insight into what stakeholders think about the district and school and the programs they offer, as well as their values, beliefs, and attitudes. This category of data can be collected through questionnaires, interviews, focus groups, and observations. All four of these measures can be collected and analyzed over time, which will provide information about changes occurring in the system.

2.2 Conduct a System Alignment Survey

The professional staff in the district and the targeted schools should now complete the System Alignment Survey. This survey is designed to elicit perceptual data about the alignment of curriculum, instruction, and assessment to state standards, as well as the availability of resources and professional development to support improvement. This information will be used later in the gap analysis.

When collecting perceptual data, ensuring confidentiality is critical so that participants are comfortable in expressing forthright and honest opinions. One way to allow for anonymity is having a survey completed online. SEDL provides an electronic version of the alignment survey online at http://www.sedl.org/ws/survey/. A survey coordinator must first go to http://www.sedl.org/ws/survey/admin/ to set up an account. This electronic format greatly expedites survey completion, as well as tabulation and summarization of the results. Reports can be generated for the district and each school completing the survey. In lieu of the online version, a printed copy of the System Alignment Survey, available in the online **Data Module,** can be printed, duplicated, and hand-scored.

In planning for administering the survey, the leadership team needs to agree on the following details:

Who will complete the survey? Every professional involved in the systemic improvement at the district level and all professional staff at the targeted schools (including administrators) should complete the survey.

What will be the deadline for completing the survey? The team needs to allow adequate time for all staff to complete the survey. It is important to identify this time frame in order to ensure that all surveys are completed before the report is generated.

How will the results be collected and analyzed? If staff complete the survey online, the results are graphed electronically. However, if the print version of the survey is used, one or more team members should be assigned to analyze and report the results. This should be done only after steps have been taken to ensure that responses remain anonymous.

2.3 Collect Additional Data From School Staff Through Interviews and Focus Groups

The primary purpose of the interviews and focus groups is to hear teachers' and other stakeholders' perceptions about initiatives, professional development, alignment, and other areas relevant to school improvement. The Conversation Guide for Interviews and Focus Groups is designed to elicit information concerning specific factors that are important to the systemic improvement.

The leadership teams should identify staff at the district and each of the targeted schools who would be most appropriate to participate in the interviews and focus groups. Interviews are usually done with individual staff; focus groups usually comprise four to six individuals.

Because confidentiality and trust are issues when sharing perceptions about district and school issues, it is often advisable to obtain the services of an outside facilitator to conduct interviews. It is also helpful for the facilitator to arrange for one or more note takers to write down teacher responses to the questions during the focus groups. This will allow the facilitator to concentrate on the questions and probes in the guide while the note takers capture as many details as possible.

The conversation guide is designed to provide the following information about how the system currently operates at the district and school levels:

- **Perceptions about the students.** Participants often reveal existing attitudes and beliefs about students in the district/school that influence decisions and actions and determine expectations for achievement outcomes. These perceptions also provide insight into the organizational and individual efficacy existing in the system to address challenging learning needs of students.

- **Current improvement programs, initiatives, or interventions.** Information and opinions about existing school improvement initiatives can help leaders determine whether any new initiative will complement those programs or compete for district resources. Existing content-area programs and initiatives may require district and school staff to spread themselves too thinly to implement the systemic work effectively. This information is important because, later in this phase, district leaders will select a focus for their improvement work.

- **Alignment of curriculum, instruction, and assessment to common core or state standards.** Descriptions of current and past efforts to align local curriculum, instruction, and assessment to standards can provide information about factors in the system that promote success and present challenges. Of particular interest are ongoing processes for supporting teachers, as well as steps taken to monitor the implementation and impact of alignment. The degree to which steps have been taken to ensure this critical alignment will be a major factor in determining initial improvement efforts.

- **Nature of professional learning.** It is useful for the leadership team to understand school leaders' awareness about the characteristics of effective professional learning and the extent to which data are used to determine professional learning needs. Participant responses will also provide information about when professional learning opportunities are available throughout the school year and the school day and reveal how well the district is guiding and supporting the implementation of new instructional strategies.

- **Opportunities for interaction and collaboration.** The team needs to know the extent to which district and school staff interact productively—both individually and organizationally—to increase student achievement. Systemic improvement requires regular and frequent collaboration among and between formal leaders and instructional staff across and within grade levels and content areas. Questions in this area are likely to reveal expectations for collaboration, how collaboration is supported and monitored, and successes and challenges in this area.

- **Communication strategies.** The manner and effectiveness in which information and priorities are communicated are important factors in shaping district and school culture. Understanding the nature of existing communication will help the leadership team maintain strategies that function well or adopt more effective ones.

- **Current structures for planning and implementing the improvement work**. Information about formal and informal structures for promoting shared decision making, identifying school priorities, using data, planning action, and monitoring implementation and impact is critical to understanding a school's context. Participant responses will reveal whether existing structures, such as district- and school-level improvement teams, are operating effectively and focused consistently on teaching and learning. The degree to which the local system is organized to increase student achievement will influence the team's choice of how to begin the improvement work.

2.4 Organize Data for Analysis

Organizing data into understandable formats enables team members to use them during the gap analysis in Step 3. District and school staff often have limited experience in examining data; therefore, the manner in which they are arrayed is critical for meaningful interpretation. The **Data Module** provides more detailed information on interpreting and displaying different types of data.

Quantitative data are usually best displayed in charts and graphs. Data that are disaggregated by demographics, content areas, and grade levels, for example, can reveal important strengths and needs in the instructional program. When collected and arrayed over time, these data can show important trends and patterns existing in the district and school.

Qualitative data, such as that collected in interviews and focus groups, can be organized by themes in response to each question in the conversation guide. The information can be incorporated into a layout similar to Themes From Interviews and Focus Groups, available in the **Data Module,** so that it may be more easily examined.

Stop and Check

Before taking the next step, make sure the following events have occurred:

✓ The leadership team has used the **Data Module** to explore types of data to collect and analyze for the CNA.

✓ The leadership team has collected student achievement, demographic, and school process data relevant to the improvement effort.

✓ The leadership team has collected perceptual data through an alignment survey, interviews, and focus groups.

✓ The data have been arrayed in an easily understood format for the leadership team to examine.

STEP 3. CONDUCT A GAP ANALYSIS

The first three parts of this step are in preparation for the fourth one: conducting a gap analysis using the System Examination Tool. This process will help the leadership team compare conditions and practices in their district and schools to those in high-performing districts and schools. The team will need to designate one or more team members to facilitate this process, or they may invite an external person to facilitate. The facilitator(s) will be responsible for gathering necessary data and other materials, creating data sets for team members, and guiding the team through the process.

> **TIP:** The decision about how much data to use in this step is largely a contextual one. In some cases, team members may already be familiar with multiple data types (e.g., student performance results, parent and community surveys) and able to synthesize information from a variety of sources. In this case, making multiple data sets available is recommended.
>
> In other cases, team members may be at the beginning stage of interpreting data. If this is true, it may be better to limit the number of data sets to be examined at any one time. The analysis process is enhanced, however, if at least two sources are reviewed; this provides an opportunity for team members to discover consistencies and inconsistencies across data sets. For example, with a novice team, one might want to begin only with student performance data in the form of state assessment results and perceptual data from student surveys. Conversations about at least two data sets often lead to questions about conflicting information, as well as additional data that have been—or should be—collected to gain a deeper understanding of conditions in the system.

3.1 Explore Predictions and Assumptions

The facilitator sets the stage for examining collected data by first surfacing what team members predict the data will reveal about their system, along with the assumptions underlying those predictions. This process helps deepen conversations during data analysis, because existing assumptions and beliefs often cause individuals to jump to unwarranted interpretations of the data. The leadership team uses the **Predictions Module,** a process adapted from Wellman and Lipton (2004), for eliciting predictions and assumptions.

3.2 Identify and Chart "Pop-Outs"

After exploring predictions and assumptions, but before examining the data accumulated up to this point (both from Phase I and II), the team reviews state and federal requirements for student proficiency under the current accountability systems. The facilitator then provides participants with student achievement data for the district and schools. It is recommended that major aspects of these data be arrayed in simple graphs to allow easy interpretation of trends. The team compares their student achievement trends to the state and national requirements as they discuss the data. Team members then use the **Pop-Outs Module** to identify issues related to alignment of curriculum, instruction, and assessment to standards or other components of the systemic work.

It should also be noted that data collection and analysis is essential throughout the process of systemic improvement. This initial analysis begins to provide a clearer picture of the current status of the district or schools. However, subsequent and ongoing data collection and analysis can probe deeper into conditions or reveal how the district and schools are progressing in their improvement efforts.

3.3 Discuss the Linkage Between Alignment and Student Achievement

A lack of alignment of curriculum, instruction, and assessment to standards is a common issue in low-performing schools. As a result, it may be useful at this point for the leadership teams to read and discuss research-based resources that highlight the importance of alignment as a means to increase student performance. Team members should understand that alignment is critical to improvement in their own district and schools, and that the improvement work is likely to require significant changes for leadership and in instructional practices.

3.4 Conduct the Gap Analysis

After acknowledging the link between alignment and student achievement, leadership team members are ready to conduct the gap analysis. The team should use the process outlined in the **Gap Analysis Module** for this step. The module contains the System Examination Tool, which is designed to help the team compare conditions and practices in their local system to those in high-performing districts and schools. The tool is divided into the eight systemic components (curriculum, instruction, assessment, standards, resources, professional staff, policy and governance, and family and community), with one page dedicated to each component. The next step, formulating a problem statement, will be based on what the team learns from practices of high-performing districts and schools on these components of the System Examination Tool.

Stop and Check

Before taking the next step, make sure the following events have occurred:

- ✓ The district leadership team has examined their predictions and assumptions regarding their collected data using the **Predictions Module.**
- ✓ The leadership team has reviewed requirements related to state and federal mandates for student achievement.
- ✓ The leadership team has used the **Pop-Outs Module** to examine student achievement data and other data to identify systemic issues in the district.
- ✓ Members of the leadership team have acknowledged the link between improving alignment and increasing student achievement.
- ✓ The leadership team has used the **Gap Analysis Module** to identify those elements in the local system that need to be strengthened during the initial improvement work.

STEP 4. BEGIN THE PROCESS AT THE SCHOOL LEVEL

4.1 Begin the Comprehensive Needs Assessment

Once the district team has completed its gap analysis, school representatives return to their respective school leadership teams and guide them as they replicate Steps 2 (Begin the Comprehensive Needs Assessment) and 3 (Conduct a Gap Analysis) for the school-level CNAs. Figure 3.2 (refer to p. 39) illustrates the sequence of the work and indicates where input to and from the district and schools contributes to the systemic process. The school leadership teams use the **Data Module** to explore categories of data and how to analyze and array data. Each team determines what data should be collected for its school in each of the four measures of data described by Bernhardt (2009). Team members at each school determine who should be included in interviews and focus groups and who should complete the System Alignment Survey. After they collect and array their data, they designate a facilitator to organize the data and prepare them for the team to review in the gap analysis.

4.2 Conduct a Gap Analysis

The school teams duplicate the process outlined in Step 3, Conduct a Gap Analysis. They first examine predictions and assumptions using the **Predictions Module** and then use the **Pop-Outs Module** to examine their accumulated data. They study and discuss resources that emphasize the linkage between alignment and student achievement and then conclude the step with the **Gap Analysis Module.** After school team members complete their gap analysis, they summarize the challenges revealed and submit the results to the district leadership team, as illustrated in Figure 3.2.

Stop and Check

Before taking the next step, make sure the following events have occurred:

✓ School leadership teams have explored data collection and analysis using the **Data Module.**

✓ School leadership teams have examined their predictions and assumptions regarding their collected data using the **Predictions Module.**

✓ School leadership teams have reviewed requirements related to state and federal mandates regarding student achievement.

✓ School leadership teams have used the **Pop-Outs Module** to examine student achievement data and other data to identify systemic issues in the school.

✓ School leadership teams have acknowledged the link between improving alignment and increasing student achievement.

Continued

Stop and Check

Continued

✓ School leadership teams have used the System Examination Tool to conduct a gap analysis and identified those elements in the local system that need to be strengthened during the initial improvement work. They have submitted their findings to the district leadership team.

STEP 5. FORMULATE PROBLEM STATEMENTS

5.1 Formulate Problem Statements Related to One or More Components of Systemic Improvement

After the school leadership teams have submitted their gap analysis findings, the district leadership team meets to review them. The team determines which of the identified school needs are appropriate to address at the district level and revises its key issues as needed. Team members discuss what those issues indicate in terms of problems that exist in the system and how these problems affect student achievement. The team consolidates the key systemic issues into one to three problem statements that will focus the initial work in the improvement plan.

The **Problem Statements Module** contains specific directions and slides for this process. The following is an example of a problem statement:

Teachers do not collaborate on lesson plans or use research-based practices, and reading instruction and assessments are not aligned to standards.

5.2 Review Research and Best Practices Directly Related to the Problem Statements

The district leadership team may find it useful to examine research and best practices relevant to the problems they just identified. This process will help the team articulate how they envision the system functioning once the problems have been addressed. The **Research Module** used in Phase III, Step 1 may be adapted for use in this step.

It is recommended that the leadership team examine current research at various points in the improvement work to ensure that they do not continue practices that have had little or no impact (or even detrimental effects) on student performance. This process could also be done after Step 6, Describe the Ideal State. It should certainly be done before developing the improvement plan so that research-based strategies and action steps can be incorporated into the document that will guide improvement efforts.

Stop and Check

Before taking the next step, make sure the following events have occurred:

✓ The district leadership team has crafted problem statements that succinctly identify the issues that the team will address in order to begin improvement work in the system.
✓ The district leadership team has ensured that the problem statements are specific enough to be manageable, yet significant enough to affect student achievement.
✓ The district leadership team has examined research and best practices related to their identified problems.

STEP 6. DESCRIBE THE IDEAL STATE

Step 6 involves a series of actions designed to help the district leadership team refine and narrow the scope of the work to make it more specific and manageable. The team should complete this step as soon as possible after formulating the problem statements and reviewing related research.

6.1 Transform the Problem Statements Into a Description of the Ideal State

The district leadership team reviews the problem statements to begin exploring the ideal state that will exist after the problems are solved. A key question to guide this discussion is, "Since the problem statements highlight the issues we want to address, how would we describe this system if the problems were completely solved?"

The team uses the process described in the **Ideal State Module** to guide development of their ideal state. The description of the ideal state should be relatively brief and focus on critical issues in the district/school. A portion of an ideal state description based on the problem statement in Step 5.1 might be the following:

Grandville School District has a system to support and ensure that teachers know and use research-based literacy practices and that they collaborate regularly to plan lessons using these practices to align instruction to state standards.

Stop and Check

Before taking the next step, make sure the following events have occurred:

✓ The district leadership team has a deeper understanding of the connections among the problem statement, the ideal state, and the components of systemic improvement.

Continued

STEP 7. REVIEW SYSTEM INITIATIVES

7.1 Review System Initiatives in Relation to Systemic Improvement

The district leadership team reviews and maps out initiatives that are in place within the district and schools. They look for inconsistencies across the system and reflect on how the various initiatives are helping them achieve the ideal state just described. They then determine which ones need to be kept or redesigned, and which can be eliminated.

7.2 Refocus on the Systemic Approach to Improvement

After reviewing existing initiatives, the leadership team refocuses on the big picture of systemic improvement. The team reflects on the interrelationships they have discovered among the components and competencies (i.e., creating coherence; collecting, interpreting, and using data; and building relationships) of the approach. Pausing to refocus and reflect on the big picture helps prevent the team from getting bogged down in minutia and keeps them focused on the overall vision for improvement.

7.3 Communicate Progress to the School Staff Involved in the Improvement Work

In systemic improvement, it is important to establish strategies for maintaining regular and effective communication between the district and school levels. Members of the district leadership team develop a plan for communicating throughout the system the progress the team has made, as well as their problem statements and description of the ideal state. This communication should include a brief outline of important findings and decisions and how they relate to specific components and competencies of the systemic improvement approach.

> **Stop and Check**
>
> *Continued*
>
> ✓ The district leadership team has refocused on the components and competencies involved in systemic improvement.
> ✓ The district leadership team has communicated its problem statements and ideal state to the participating schools.
> ✓ The district leadership team has developed and implemented a plan for communicating its findings, decisions, and progress throughout the local system.

STEP 8. CONTINUE THE PROCESS AT THE SCHOOL LEVEL

School representatives on the district team return to their schools to guide their school leadership team through formulating their own problem statements and describing the ideal state. The district-team representatives should be ready to respond to questions about the district's problem statements and ideal state and address any concerns expressed at the school level. Any issues that arise can be taken back to the district leadership team for further discussion, if appropriate.

8.1 Formulate Problem Statements

The school leadership teams replicate Step 5, using the **Problem Statements Module** to identify problems existing in their respective schools. Team members should keep in mind the district's problem statements and ideal state description as they complete this activity. This will help ensure that the district and school improvement efforts are aligned and mutually supportive. However, school teams should not merely replicate the district's problem statements. Rather, they must formulate problem statements that address the most important problems hindering student achievement in the context of their own schools.

School teams may then adapt the **Research Module** from Phase III, Step 1, to review research-based practices related to their identified problems. This will enable them to describe their ideal state in terms of practices that have been shown to have a positive effect on student performance.

8.2 Describe Ideal State

Each school leadership team describes what its school will be like after the identified problems are solved. To do this, the teams use the **Ideal State Module** and duplicate the process used by the district leadership team in Step 6.

8.3 Review System Initiatives

Each school leadership team reviews current school-level initiatives related to the ideal state (as in Step 7.1) and refocuses on their role as part of the systemic improvement process (as in Step 7.2). These actions help determine whether local initiatives are likely to assist the school in reaching the ideal state or hinder the systemic effort. They also help broaden commitment to the total improvement effort.

Stop and Check

Before taking the next step, make sure the following events have occurred:

- ✓ School leadership teams have used the **Problem Statements Module** to identify the major problems that need to be addressed in the schools.
- ✓ School leadership teams have used the **Ideal State Module** to transform problem statements into descriptions of ideal states that would be achieved if the problems were completely solved.
- ✓ School leadership teams have reviewed system initiatives and determined how they contribute to the school's improvement effort.

Vignette

PHASE II AT GRANDVILLE SCHOOL DISTRICT AND DELIGHTFUL INTERMEDIATE SCHOOL

Form the District and School Leadership Teams

Superintendent Dunbar and the key leaders recognize that this systemic improvement effort will require strong leadership across the district. She and her key leaders work together to determine who should be members of their district leadership team. They identify Dr. Dunbar; the district directors of curriculum, federal programs, and special education; the principals from each school in the district; one parent; one board member; and two teachers from each of the two schools participating in the systemic improvement effort.

At the initial district leadership team meeting, the members immediately begin to explore their student achievement data. Unfortunately, principals and teachers become defensive about instances of low performance and the tone of the meeting takes a negative turn. Team members begin to attribute blame to parents, students, and a lack of resources. Two team members monopolize the discussion and two other team members engage in frequent side conversations with one another. The meeting ends with all team members frustrated and confused.

Dr. Dunbar goes back to her office to study the process for systemic improvement and discovers that she omitted an important step after forming the leadership team—establishing norms and guidelines. At the next meeting, these two tasks are placed at the beginning of the agenda.

Meanwhile, at Delightful School, Mr. Martinez consults with his assistant principal and counselor in organizing his leadership team. In addition to Mr. Martinez, members of the school team include one teacher from each grade level, two parents, a community social worker, the school counselor, the computer science teacher, the special education teacher, and the ELL specialist.

Begin the Comprehensive Needs Assessment

After the district leadership team reconvenes and develops norms and guidelines for meetings, they reexamine the student achievement reports that they attempted to analyze at the previous meeting. They discover that it is difficult to interpret the student achievement reports in their current format. Federal programs director Sandra Cox, who is very computer-savvy, volunteers to display the data in graphs and tables for the next meeting.

Dr. Dunbar also notes that although annual reports of student performance on the state test provide a picture of past and current status, they offer no insight into the underlying factors affecting student achievement. The superintendent introduces different types of data that could be collected to provide more information about underlying causal factors. The team decides to have the staff respond to the System Alignment Survey and participate in interviews and focus groups. They set a deadline for completion of the data collection and schedule the analysis of these data for the next meeting. Before adjourning, team members agree that the interactions among team members have significantly improved, and the meeting was much more productive.

Conduct a Gap Analysis

At the next meeting, before examining the graphs of data prepared by Federal Programs Director Cox, the district leadership team takes a few minutes to predict what the data will reveal about their system. Team members predict that overall reading achievement, and particularly achievement of Hispanic students, has improved because of a districtwide reading initiative that was adopted two years ago. They also predict that because teachers received professional development when the initiative was adopted, almost all teachers are fully implementing the teaching strategies that are essential components of the reading initiative. Finally, they predict that all teachers understand and regularly use the district reading curriculum.

Upon examination of the data, interesting information pops out that contradicts the team's predictions. They learn that achievement of Hispanic students has actually declined over the last three years. The System Alignment Survey and focus group data show that not all teachers are implementing the teaching strategies in the district reading initiative, particularly those teachers new to the district. They also learn that some teachers have never accessed the district reading curriculum and are using their textbooks rather than the district curriculum to guide instruction. These discoveries lead the team to question their assumptions that curriculum, instruction, and assessment are truly aligned to state standards.

After examining their data, the district team reviews the eight components of systemic improvement in the System Examination Tool. In this process, the team compares the local system to indicators of high-performing systems in two of the eight areas—instruction and professional staff. They find that there is insufficient support to ensure that instruction is of high quality and that the teachers receive insufficient professional development to implement research-based practices effectively. Knowing they still have much to learn about the linkage between alignment and student achievement, they locate and study three research articles to help them better understand why this linkage is so important.

Begin the Process at the School Level

In order to ensure that the process becomes systemic, school representatives from the district leadership team use the processes that the district leadership team used to establish norms, examine data, and conduct a gap analysis in their respective schools.

Mr. Martinez recalls the unsatisfactory outcomes from the first district leadership team meeting and decides to open his initial school team meeting by engaging team members in establishing their own roles, norms, and operating guidelines. This seems to get the team off to a good start.

The experiences that the district team had help to guide Mr. Martinez in carrying out the processes for productive data dialogue and exploration of practices in high-performing systems. He explores systemic improvement with his team and distributes two articles on systemic reform for the team to read before the next meeting. He also emphasizes the importance of leadership on the part of formal and informal leaders. He particularly stresses the team's role in establishing effective communication between the team members and other staff members, as well as the community.

Team members schedule monthly meetings for the remainder of the school year before they adjourn.

At the next meeting of Delightful's leadership team, Mr. Martinez begins the meeting with a discussion of the articles distributed at the previous meeting. Although team members are reluctant at first to express their reactions to the articles, they become more comfortable as the discussion goes on. Mr. Martinez deems this as an important first step in transforming his school into a community of professional learners.

As the team examines Delightful's student achievement data, members recall that three years ago, Delightful School was identified as low performing by the state's accountability system for both reading and math. Last year it was one of three schools in the district that failed to meet the state improvement standards in reading. They learn that students receiving special education services did not meet the improvement standard for reading performance. Students identified as English language learners (ELLs) did not meet the standard for reading two years ago but showed considerable improvement *this past year. Even so, they were barely above this year's state standard. Although most students met the state standard last year, there were across-the-board declines in academic achievement for reading compared to the previous year, except for the ELLs mentioned above. Math scores have been relatively constant for the past three years.*

The leadership team members acknowledge that Mr. Martinez spends many long hours at the school exploring a number of options to increase student achievement. Still, he, and they, can't explain why the students are not performing better. In interviews and focus groups, the Delightful staff indicate that they work hard and want their students to be successful. But, like the principal, they are not able to determine why scores are dropping for most student groups. They seem to have difficulty describing specific district or school initiatives that have been adopted to address the areas of need.

After going through the processes of data examination and the gap analysis, the school leadership team discovers that Delightful School needs additional support in the areas of effective instructional strategies and professional development, as the district does. In addition, they discover that the school's parental involvement efforts have been generally unsuccessful.

Mr. Martinez, and the two school representatives to the district team, Tonya Sykes and Gail Perkins, plan how to share findings from Delightful's data examination and gap analysis with the district team. Mr. Martinez is pleased that the two teacher representatives volunteer to make this report to the district team, an indication that they are beginning to assume greater leadership responsibilities. The reports from Delightful and Fairview Elementary, the other school selected for the initial systemic improvement work, will help inform the district team on whether or not the district findings are also reflected in the school-level findings.

Formulate Problem Statements

From the information analyzed in the comprehensive needs assessment, as well as the information provided from Delightful and Fairview schools, the district leadership team develops a problem statement that reflects what they believe is the most significant issue affecting student performance.

> The district does not have a system that ensures teachers have access to and use the district curriculum that is aligned to state standards, and the district does not allocate sufficient time for staff collaboration to align instruction to the curriculum. The district does not have a plan for providing teachers professional development on the use of research-based literacy practices.

The district leadership team then locates and studies research-based articles that provide information on how teams of teachers can improve instructional practices through collaboration. They also study current research on instructional practices that are highly associated with increased student learning. They learn that literacy instruction should be a part of every subject area and that all teachers need to be aware of effective literacy practices for their own content areas. While examining research seemed to be a time-consuming endeavor at first, the process makes the team much more aware of what is missing in their district and steps they can take to improve student learning.

Describe the Ideal State

Using the information learned from the research articles, the district team formulates an ideal state that describes the local system once the problem is solved.

All teachers in the district have access to and use the district curriculum, which is aligned to standards, to guide their instructional practices. The district allocates sufficient time and professional development for teachers to work in collaborative teams and align their instruction to the curriculum using research-based literacy practices.

Review System Initiatives

Through a review of system initiatives, the district leadership team members realize that they have attempted to implement three major reading initiatives over the past five years. However, the team is unsure which, if any, of the initiatives are being fully implemented as designed and whether they are resulting in increased student performance. In fact, some components of the three reading initiatives appear to conflict with one another and compete for instructional time and resources. Through their study of systemic improvement, the team understands that the initiatives must be complementary to address identified needs.

Team members are eager to share with others what they've learned as a district team. They plan how they will report their progress and the status of their work to schools, their parent/teacher organization, the community, and the school board. Mr. Martinez asks the two district team members from Delightful to lead a discussion of the research articles back at Delightful, and the Fairview principal asks his team representatives to do the same. Other district leadership team members express interest in sharing the articles with their colleagues as well.

Continue the Process at the School Level

At Delightful, Mark Martinez convenes a meeting of the school leadership team to report the progress of the district team. The two district team representatives from Delightful lead a successful discussion of the research articles on literacy instruction and collaboration. This information sets the stage for formulating the problem statement and describing the ideal state at the school.

Mr. Martinez then shares the district's problem statement and ideal state so that the school team can consider how these issues manifest themselves at the school level. As the principal and his teacher representatives lead the school team in formulating the school's problem statements, they determine that, in addition to the district's problem, Delightful staff have significant challenges with family and community involvement. As a result, they formulate the following problem statements:

Teachers do not collaborate on lesson plans or use research-based practices, and literacy instruction is not aligned to standards.

Staff, family, and community members do not participate in decision making about issues that affect student learning.

Before the next school leadership team meeting, members explore research on family and community involvement. The team then works together to describe an ideal state for Delightful school:

Teachers attend professional development on research-based literacy practices, and they apply their learning as they collaboratively plan instruction aligned to state standards. The school provides meaningful opportunities for staff, families, and the community to participate in decision making affecting student learning.

As the team examines their current literacy initiatives, they are pleased to find that they have several initiatives in place to address the students' reading performance. However, Tonya Sykes, one of Delightful's teacher representatives to the district team, challenges them to identify evidence that the initiatives are being implemented as designed and are having the desired impact. Furthermore, she questions whether teachers hired in the last two years have ever received professional development on the reading initiatives. Team members begin to understand why their past improvement efforts have been unsuccessful and are already thinking about how they might focus their improvement plan next year.

Additional materials and resources related to *Getting Serious About the System* can be found at http://www.corwin.com/gettingserious

4

Phase III

Planning Action

Planning Action is the third of five phases in systemic improvement. In the first two phases, Understanding Systemic Improvement and Analyzing the System, district leaders examined the new approach and reviewed data about their system. Leaders used this information as the basis for a decision to commit to implementing a long-term improvement process designed to raise student achievement. They selected the participating schools and organized district and school leadership teams that are representative of the levels of the local system (district, school, and classroom) to oversee the improvement effort. The leadership teams then completed a series of steps in which they became progressively more specific in describing the system's problems to be addressed and the ideal state to be achieved. This prior work will serve as the foundation for the improvement plans to be developed during Phase III.

In Planning Action, leaders reflect on what research shows to be effective practices for increasing student achievement and consider how those practices can be incorporated into the improvement effort. The teams gain more insight into the status of their district's and schools' existing improvement plans and the process used to develop them. Leaders develop detailed plans that lay out the goals, objectives, strategies, and action steps, as well as the necessary monitoring and support.

Planning Action consists of six steps:

Step 1. Investigate Research-Based Practices. The leadership team reviews research about practices to improve teaching and learning. Although the review of research is tailored to the specific needs of the school system, it should initially center on three topic areas vital to improving student learning:

- Alignment of curriculum, instruction, and assessment to standards
- Ongoing, job-embedded professional development
- Leadership roles to support implementation

Additional conversation occurs about characteristics of low-performing schools and the extent to which these characteristics are apparent in the local system.

Step 2. Explore the Professional Teaching and Learning Cycle (PTLC). The leadership team explores the PTLC as a strategy for ensuring alignment through ongoing, job-embedded professional development. The team focuses on the leadership roles, culture, and conditions that support implementation of the PTLC.

Step 3. Review Progress Made to Date and Existing Plan. A review of the outcomes of previous phases of the work is useful in keeping the leadership team's focus on the big picture of the improvement effort. It is also helpful to review the existing plan in order to determine whether it contains any strategies or action steps that address the identified problems. This examination may also reveal whether the plan is well designed for implementation (e.g., contains actionable strategies and steps and processes for monitoring).

Step 4. Develop a District Improvement Plan. The district leadership team develops an improvement plan that is specifically focused on addressing the identified systemic problems. The team establishes goals, objectives, strategies, and action steps designed to help the district achieve its ideal state; explores leadership roles needed to support the plan's implementation; and develops processes and procedures for monitoring and making adjustments as needed.

Step 5. Formalize and Communicate the District Improvement Plan. Communicating key aspects of the improvement plan helps those involved, both directly and indirectly, to understand the nature and extent of the improvement work. The leadership team prepares a presentation, first for the school board and then the staff at participating schools. These presentations provide opportunities for others to ask questions and obtain clarification about the plan.

Step 6. Develop School Improvement Plans. In this step, the planning stage of the work moves to the school level. Each school leadership team replicates Phase III, Steps 1–4 to develop a plan that addresses their own identified needs. They ensure that the school's plan is aligned with the district's plan and that the two plans are mutually supportive. The teams submit the completed plans to the district team for review.

Once the Planning Action phase of the work is completed, leaders and staff members at all levels will have detailed plans that map out the work ahead and the tools necessary for implementing and monitoring the work in the next phase.

Figure 4.1 Competencies Developed in Phase III

PHASE	Competencies				
	Coherence	Data	Professional Learning	Relationships	Change
Phase III: Planning Action Purpose: Explore research-based strategies for providing quality learning for all and consider how actions can be incorporated into improvement plans; develop or revise improvement plan	X	X	X		X

In Phase III, district- and school-level leaders build their competencies, particularly in creating coherence; collecting, interpreting, and using data; and building relationships (see Figure 4.1). By concentrating on these competencies throughout this phase of the work, leaders apply newly acquired skills to real-life situations in systemic improvement.

STEP 1. INVESTIGATE RESEARCH-BASED PRACTICES

1.1 Review Research on Effective Practices for Improving Teaching and Learning

In this step, leaders become aware of research-based and promising practices. These are practices used by high-performing systems to ensure that well-developed improvement plans are implemented at all levels of the system and that the plans have a positive impact on student achievement. The leadership team may have investigated research after formulating the problem statements in Phase II. If not, or if it was done only minimally, it is important that the team look carefully at research and best practices at this point—before developing the improvement plan. Team members need to know what practices have been shown by research to improve student performance and to incorporate into their plan those practices that may help in solving the problems they have identified.

The **Research Module** guides the leadership team through an examination of research on professional learning. But the process can be adapted to use with any topic. Pertinent areas of research include the following:

- **Alignment of curriculum, instruction, and assessment to standards.** Because alignment is a school-level factor highly associated with increased student achievement, it should be an initial consideration for school improvement.

- **Ongoing, job-embedded professional learning.** Professional learning should not be a one-time event that occurs isolated from any ongoing effort; it is an integral part of systemic change. It must be ongoing, standards based, and results driven.
- **Leadership roles to support implementation.** Leadership at all levels of the system must support implementation of new practices. Effective leaders assume responsibility for communicating clear expectations, building capacity, and monitoring and reviewing.

Leading researchers suggest that a collaborative process for alignment and job-embedded professional learning is a critical aspect of school improvement. It would be helpful to have available some examples of the research literature on this topic. It may also be useful to review some of the resources describing the importance of looking at student work. This information prepares the team to explore the Professional Teaching and Learning Cycle in the following step. The Bibliography Matrix at the back of the book gives some suggestions for exploring these topics.

1.2 Discuss Characteristics of Low-Performing Districts and Schools

The leadership team can also examine the following list of characteristics of low-performing districts/schools and then discuss the extent to which they are apparent in the local system:

- Extremely low standards and expectations for students
- Very little use of data to identify and solve specific problems
- Limited capacity for implementing improvement efforts
- Inadequate knowledge of quality instruction
- Less experienced and less qualified teachers and other instructional staff
- High staff absenteeism and turnover rates
- Inadequate leadership for substantive change
- Atmosphere of distrust, disrespect, and barely controlled chaos
- Low morale

Chenowith (2007), Cohen & Ginsburg (2001), and Corallo & McDonald (2002)

Stop and Check

Before taking the next step, make sure the following events have occurred:

✓ The leadership team has reviewed research on effective practices for teaching and learning.
✓ The team has discussed the characteristics of low-performing districts and schools in relation to their own system.

STEP 2. EXPLORE THE PROFESSIONAL TEACHING AND LEARNING CYCLE (PTLC)

2.1 Examine the PTLC as a Strategy for Ongoing, Job-Embedded Professional Learning

The PTLC provides a process for creating (or strengthening) a professional learning community (PLC) among the instructional staff. It is designed to promote a critical aspect of improving student outcomes—the alignment of curriculum, instruction, and assessment to standards—through the examination of research-based instructional practices and student work. It offers a structure for collaboration about teaching and learning and also promotes continuous, job-embedded professional learning. High levels of student performance become the ultimate shared goals, and strong professional relationships support continuous inquiry about existing and new instructional practices.

> **TIP:** The similarity between the acronyms, PTLC and PLC, may be somewhat confusing. The PTLC (Professional Teaching and Learning Cycle) is a process implemented by a school that helps them operate as a PLC (professional learning community).

The PTLC is a lesson-study process and a valuable strategy for extending the systemic work to the classroom level. It must be emphasized, however, that while PTLC is one way to do lesson study, it is only one of several methods that may be used by a school to improve instruction and assessment.

2.2 Explore the Steps of the PTLC

The **PTLC Module** provides a process for introducing its purpose and exploring the steps of the PTLC. The process begins with an examination of data to identify a specific content-area focus. An item analysis of student achievement results can provide information about which of the specific learning expectations within the common core or state standards should be addressed first. Then the six steps below are followed:

- Step 1. Study
  Teachers work in collaborative planning teams (grade level, vertical, or departmental) to examine the learning expectations from the selected standards; they also review how those expectations are assessed on the state assessment.
- Step 2. Select
  Collaborative planning teams research and select instructional strategies and resources for enhancing learning as described in the standards.
- Step 3. Plan
  Planning teams, working together, develop a common lesson incorporating the selected strategies, and they agree on the type of student work teachers will use as evidence of student learning in Step 5 (Analyze).

- Step 4. Implement
  Teachers teach the planned lesson, making note of implementation successes and challenges, and gather the agreed-upon evidence of student learning.
- Step 5. Analyze
  Teachers meet again in collaborative teams to examine student work and reflect on student performance as an indicator of instructional effectiveness.
- Step 6. Adjust
  Collaborative teams reflect on the implications of the analysis of student work. Teachers discuss alternative instructional strategies or modifications to the original instructional strategy that would enhance student learning.

2.3 Investigate the Leadership Roles to Support Implementation of the PTLC

The PTLC requires three leadership roles to support implementation: communicating clear expectations, building capacity, and monitoring and reviewing. The following is a brief synopsis of the leadership roles; Figure 4.2 provides a graphic representation of how those roles and the PTLC fit together within a culture that is supportive of the process (Cowan, 2009; Tobia, 2007).

Communicating Clear Expectations

- Regularly communicates expectations in both words and actions
- Frequently expresses the priorities related to student achievement to a wide audience
- Actively participates in meetings and professional learning sessions to convey their importance and value

Building Capacity

- Supports collaborative learning at all levels of the system
- Provides time, space, and resources needed for staff to learn how to increase student learning
- Regularly engages in personal professional learning for effective teaching and learning

Monitoring and Reviewing

- Regularly and frequently monitors implementation and impact of initiatives
- Engages others in collecting and analyzing data to assess implementation and impact of improvement initiatives
- Regularly and frequently uses different forms of data to make decisions

Leadership actions for supporting implementation of the PTLC should be included in the improvement plan. The **Leadership Module** that will be

Figure 4.2 The PTLC Steps, Leadership Roles, and Culture

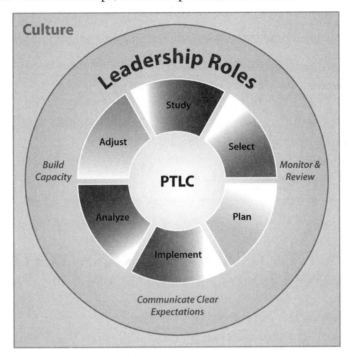

used in Step 4.3 contains tools that the team can use periodically to monitor leadership actions. Additional information on leadership roles is provided in Phase IV, Step 2.

2.4 Consider the Culture and Conditions Necessary to Support the PTLC

A collaborative culture at all levels of the system is vital to the implementation of the PTLC. The process requires teachers to engage in frequent meetings with grade-level or content-area colleagues in which they critically examine their instructional practices and explore more effective teaching strategies. The PTLC also requires a strong commitment to the process on the part of leaders. Several considerations are important in determining the district's/school's capacity to support the PTLC, including the extent to which

- the district and schools demonstrate a sense of urgency about the need for instructional improvement,
- an environment of collaboration and trust exists in the district and schools,
- teachers are willing to examine their own instructional practices,
- teachers are open to trying new instructional strategies,
- district and school leaders are willing to monitor and support implementation of the PTLC, and
- the district and schools encourage a sense of mutual responsibility and accountability.

Stop and Check

Before taking the next step, make sure the following events have occurred:

✓ The leadership team has examined the PTLC as an ongoing, job-embedded strategy for professional development and instructional alignment.

✓ The leadership team has completed the **PTLC Module** to explore the purpose, steps, and necessary culture for the PTLC.

✓ The leadership team has investigated three leadership roles to support implementation of the PTLC.

STEP 3. REVIEW PROGRESS MADE TO DATE AND EXISTING PLAN

3.1 Review the Outcomes of the First Two Phases of the Work

The district leadership team reviews the accomplishments and decisions made in the first two phases. This is particularly important if significant time has lapsed between the completion of the previous phase of the work and this point in the process. This information will guide development of the improvement plan.

The review includes the following points:

- A summary of the collected data
- The outcomes of the gap analysis
- The team's problem statements
- The ideal state

3.2 Review the Existing Improvement Plan

The leadership team uses the **Existing Plan Module** to examine the current improvement plan and the extent to which it is designed to solve the problems identified in Phase II. The review should also reveal the district's and schools' past successes in implementing and monitoring its plans. If the plan is lengthy, the team should direct its initial attention only to those parts of the plan that are directly related to student learning.

The team will discuss the following questions when reviewing the plan:

- **How was the plan developed?** This information will reveal the extent to which the district and school improvement plans were collaboratively developed. It should also bring out information about whether data were used to identify district and school needs and whether the planning was a deliberative process, or was done only to satisfy state or federal requirements.

- **Does the plan map out a clear course of action centered on using research-based practices?** The team examines the extent to which the plan reflects research-based strategies and provides clear direction about who will take which actions and by when.

- **Does the plan identify professional learning required for implementation?** The team discusses whether the district and schools developed a process for identifying the skills and knowledge that staff members need in order to implement actions in the improvement plan. The team also determines to what degree the district and schools have followed through and provided for those needs.

- **Does the plan allocate sufficient resources for priorities and initiatives?** The team determines whether the district and schools have provided adequate resources (e.g., time, money, and staff) to address identified needs and implement multiple priorities and initiatives effectively.

- **Is there a process for monitoring the implementation and impact of strategies?** The team reflects on the district's and schools' history of implementing improvement plans and determines whether the current plan includes a clear process for regularly checking on progress in carrying out the actions in the plan. This process should include a specific timeline for monitoring both implementation and impact of individual strategies. The team identifies the data sources used to measure whether the strategies were implemented and whether they achieved desired outcomes.

The leadership team also analyzes how the plan addresses issues related to the problem statements and ideal state developed in Phase II. Parts of the current plan that are relevant to the identified problems might be modified or strengthened during the development of the new improvement plan. The **Existing Plan Module** contains a tool that can be used to assess the existing plan in relation to the big ideas contained in the ideal state described at the end of Phase II.

Stop and Check

Before taking the next step, make sure the following events have occurred:

- ✓ The leadership team has reviewed outcomes of the first two phases of the work.
- ✓ The leadership team has reviewed the current improvement plan in relation to the problem statements and the ideal state.

STEP 4. DEVELOP A DISTRICT IMPROVEMENT PLAN

4.1 Establish Goals and Objectives to Reach the Ideal State

In the previous step, the leadership team familiarized itself with the development and content of the existing plan and its likelihood for moving the district toward its ideal state. To begin the process of developing (or revising) an improvement plan, the team members review their problem statements and confirm the ideal state they have described. These are then used to identify the goals and objectives that will serve as the framework for the plan. As a rule of thumb, the leadership team should establish one or two goals that address the most important issues that surfaced during the gap analysis. For each goal, the team creates one to three objectives that will lead to attaining that goal. The **Goals and Objectives Module** guides the team through this process. Figure 4.3 shows how the goals and objectives relate to the strategies and action steps that will be determined in the next step.

4.2 Establish Strategies and Actions to Achieve the Objectives

The team next uses the **Strategies and Actions Module** to complete the improvement plan. In addition to outlining the process for developing strategies and action steps, this module helps the team determine

(for each strategy)

- what evidence will demonstrate that the strategy was completed (evidence of implementation),
- what evidence will demonstrate that the strategy had any effect on moving toward the ideal state (evidence of impact),

(for each action step)

- the person(s) ultimately responsible for carrying out each action step,
- resources needed to implement the action step,
- the date by which the step should be completed, and
- a timeline that specifies when the action step will be reviewed.

As the team members develop their improvement plan later in this phase, they should incorporate action steps to implement the PTLC. Processes for monitoring implementation of each step of the PTLC should be included in the plan. The **PTLC Module** provides a Professional Teaching and Learning Cycle Rubric that the leadership team can periodically use to monitor implementation.

4.3 Explore Leadership Roles

It is important for the team to remember the three leadership roles—communicate clear expectations, build capacity, monitor and review—

Figure 4.3 GOSA Chart (Goal, Objectives, Strategies, Action Steps)

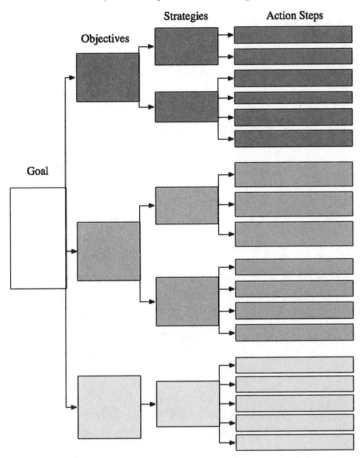

discussed in Step 2.3 as necessary for implementing the PTLC. These same leadership roles are needed to support implementation of the improvement plan.

Communicate Clear Expectations

Keeping the goals and work of the improvement effort a priority at all levels of the system is critical for achieving success. District and school leaders should

- communicate clearly that the work is—and will remain—a priority;
- keep the work of the improvement effort continuous; and
- keep the improvement effort central to the team's focus.

Build Capacity

District and school leaders take action to ensure that staff members develop the knowledge and skills they need in order to succeed in the necessary tasks. Leaders should

- ensure that staff members develop and apply needed knowledge and skills to carry out the improvement work successfully and
- ensure that the required resources, including time and staff, are available to meet the identified needs of the system.

Monitor and Review

Monitoring implementation and impact of the planned work is a critical part of the improvement effort. Reviewing progress on a regular basis helps guide decisions about how best to direct and support the endeavor. District and school leaders should

- design a system to monitor implementation of the improvement plan and its impact on student achievement and
- confer on a regular basis with individuals carrying out the improvement plan and work proactively to address issues that arise.

The team studies the descriptions of the leadership roles and uses the tools in the **Leadership Module.** These tools can be used to guide the team in determining specific leadership action steps for the improvement plan and in identifying where leadership capacity must be built to carry out the plan. These actions may best be added after the rest of the plan is complete.

The **Leadership Module** can also be used by leaders to examine their strengths and weaknesses in the identified roles. Maintaining a copy of the completed Leadership Self-Assessment tool and reflecting on it at intervals throughout the year can help leaders monitor their own growth in the three leadership roles.

4.4 Establish Processes and Procedures for Making Revisions to the Improvement Plan, as Needed

The team identifies specific dates for reviewing the improvement plan, particularly the evidence of implementation and impact. It is recommended that the team review the plan at least quarterly. As the plan is being implemented and monitored, the leadership team may see the need for adjustments. In some cases, action steps in the original plan will need to be revised; in other cases, steps may need to be deleted, added, or extended in time. These changes need to be noted in the plan during the reviews and communicated throughout the system. The Improvement Plan Revision Form in Phase IV (Figure 5.3 in Chapter 5) provides an example of a document to help track changes to the plan. This process ensures that the improvement plan will remain a living document that actively guides the work.

4.5 Incorporate Important Milestones and Dates Into the District Calendar

A key step in planning the improvement work is to place important items from the plan on the district and school calendar for the year ahead. Possible events to be scheduled include the following:

- Monthly meetings of the leadership team
- Regular reviews of the improvement plan
- Progress updates to schools
- Professional development sessions

Stop and Check

Before taking the next step, make sure the following events have occurred:

✓ The district leadership team has completed the **Goals and Objectives Module**.

✓ The district leadership team has completed the **Strategies and Action Steps Module**.

✓ The district leadership team has completed the **Leadership Module** and has a clear understanding of the importance of monitoring the implementation and impact of strategies in the improvement plan.

✓ The leadership team has established processes and procedures for reviewing and revising the improvement plan, as needed.

✓ The leadership team has incorporated important milestones and dates into the district and school calendar.

STEP 5. FORMALIZE AND COMMUNICATE THE DISTRICT IMPROVEMENT PLAN

5.1 Present the District Plan to the School Board

It is important for the school board, as the governing body of the school district, to understand the nature and extent of the work to be undertaken in the implementation of the district improvement plan. The school board can be instrumental in setting policies, ensuring that needed resources are available, and communicating the district focus to the larger community. The district team prepares and presents the finalized plan to the school board. A summary of the district team's comprehensive needs assessment, the problem statements, and the ideal state should be included in this presentation, as well as a brief explanation of the following key points:

- How the plan was developed with input from staff members at all levels of the local system
- How the district plan will be implemented
- How the district will keep the improvement effort a long-term priority
- How school improvement plans will be developed
- How district and school plans will be mutually supportive

5.2 Present the District Plan to the School Staff

Although a school leadership team will guide the improvement efforts at the school level, all staff need to be aware of the district plan. District-team representatives from each of the participating schools determine how to communicate the district improvement plan to their respective school staff. In addition to the key points provided to the school board, the following information should be communicated in this meeting:

- Explanation of how needs/challenges identified by the participating schools were taken into consideration in developing the district plan
- Emphasis that implementation of the district and school plans will be a priority at the district level, demonstrating that the system is taking proactive steps to improve student achievement and serve all of the students in the district
- Summary of the next steps that will occur, primarily the development of the school improvement plan
- Recognition of school representatives on the district leadership team, reinforcing that representation from all levels of the local system was instrumental in the plan development

Stop and Check

Before taking the next step, make sure the following events have occurred:

✓ The district leadership team has presented the district improvement plan to the school board.
✓ The school representatives on the district leadership team have presented the district improvement plan to staff at their respective participating schools.

STEP 6. DEVELOP SCHOOL IMPROVEMENT PLANS

6.1 Develop a School Improvement Plan

A key aspect of creating coherence in a system is ensuring that improvement plans at the district and school levels are mutually supportive. Each school leadership team reviews its ideal state and determines whether revisions are needed so that the school's improvement work supports the district's priorities. The school team then develops its own improvement plan—following the procedure described in Phase III, Steps 1 through 4. Although Step 4 is titled "Develop a District Improvement Plan," the process described is also used to develop the school plan. During the development of the school plan, the team consults the district plan to ensure alignment of the two plans.

Of critical importance is the understanding that meaningful change in student performance will not occur until the improvement work reaches the classroom level. Also, as in the district plan, monitoring implementation and impact of strategies is crucial and must not be omitted from the plan.

Once the school improvement plan has been completed, the leadership team submits the plan to the district leadership team for review. If no revisions are suggested, the school team may continue with the next step, presenting the plan to the school staff.

6.2 Present the School Plan to the School Staff

The leadership team decides how to communicate the details of the school improvement plan to teachers and other staff members at the school and classroom levels. It is important for all staff to recognize that the school plan and the district plan are mutually supportive. Another key point should be the collaborative nature of the plan development, with input provided from school-level staff in the development of the district's improvement plan as well as their own.

Leaders should emphasize that implementation of both the district and school plans will be given high priority at appropriate levels of the system and also that active participation by all staff will be expected and encouraged. Finally, the team should explain what the next steps will be in implementing the plan.

Stop and Check

Before taking the next step, make sure the following events have occurred:

✓ Each school leadership team has developed an improvement plan aligned to the district improvement plan, using the **Goals and Objectives Module** and the **Strategies and Action Steps Module.**

✓ Each school leadership team has completed the **Leadership Module** and has a clear understanding of the importance of monitoring and accountability in successfully implementing the improvement plan.

✓ School improvement plans have been submitted to and reviewed by the district leadership team.

✓ Each school leadership team has presented its improvement plan to the school staff.

Vignette

PHASE III AT GRANDVILLE SCHOOL DISTRICT AND DELIGHTFUL INTERMEDIATE SCHOOL

Investigate Research-Based Practices

Although Grandville's district leadership team has begun to learn about what high-performing systems do by conducting a gap analysis, they determine that they need further information about how to improve instruction and collaboration throughout the district. Because implementation of the existing reading initiatives has been inconsistent, they attribute their lack of success to insufficient opportunities for meaningful professional learning and collaboration.

Superintendent Dunbar locates three articles for the team to study that address high-quality, job-embedded professional learning. After studying the research, team members feel that they have a much better understanding of what needs to be done to provide high-quality professional development in the district. The articles especially help them realize the need to provide protected time for teachers to collaborate regularly to align their instruction to state standards and plan high-quality lessons. They also note the need for leadership to monitor the implementation and impact of professional development.

Explore the PTLC

In response to the need for effective professional learning opportunities, Curriculum Director Oscar Franklin introduces the team to the Professional Teaching and Learning Cycle (PTLC), a lesson study process that promotes alignment of curriculum, instruction, and assessments to state standards; productive collaboration; and implementation of research-based instructional strategies through on-going, job-embedded professional development.

After exploring each of the six steps in the PTLC, the team seems enthusiastic but also recognizes that it will require many changes in how the Grandville District teachers interact. At the current time, there is a lack of professional respect and trust among many teachers. Gail Perkins, one of Delightful's teacher representatives to the district team, expresses concern about the amount of time required for collaboration, leaving her even less time than she has now to plan her own lessons. Mr. Martinez tries to clarify that one important aspect of PTLC implementation is to plan common lessons. While these meetings may take more time initially as they are learning the process, they will ultimately save time as teachers share ideas for creating effective lessons. Based on what she remembers about past initiatives in the district, Ms. Perkins is not altogether convinced, but is willing to give it a try. The team agrees that they will need to work together to ensure the support and resources the teachers will need to implement the PTLC.

Review Progress Made to Date and the Existing Plan

Before preparing a plan to address their newly identified needs, leadership team members examine their existing plan to determine whether any of the strategies or actions should be continued or perhaps revised to meet these needs. The team knows that some of its past efforts have been successful in addressing identified needs. For example, having recently studied their data on students participating in the district math tutoring program, they found that the program was well implemented and was producing positive achievement outcomes for students. For this reason, the team decides to extend the tutoring program to additional students.

On the other hand, they discover that only one of the three existing reading initiatives is showing any measure of success. They decide to eliminate the other two reading initiatives and focus more on the implementation of the successful one. In addition, many of the strategies and action steps in their current plan were not implemented and do not really reflect the research-based strategies described in the articles they read. Furthermore, they note that a great number of the strategies and action steps do not address the needs they just identified in the needs assessment. The team decides to remove these from next year's plan.

Develop a District Improvement Plan

Using the description of the ideal state as a starting point, the district leadership team establishes goals and objectives that will serve as the framework for the improvement plan. They recall their ideal state:

All teachers in the district have access to and use the district curriculum (aligned to state standards) to guide their instructional practices. The district allocates sufficient time and professional development for teachers to collaboratively align their instruction to the curriculum using research-based literacy practices.

From this statement, they are able to identify goals that will help them reach their ideal state. They make sure that each of the goals is specific, measurable, attainable, relevant, and time bound (SMART). The team develops its first SMART goal:

By the end of the current year, 100% of teachers will know and use at least four research-based literacy practices and they will collaborate monthly to align instruction to the district curriculum.

The team then proceeds to identify three objectives for meeting the goal:

The district will provide professional development on four research-based literacy practices.

The district will provide time for teachers to collaboratively plan lessons incorporating the four research-based practices.

The district will monitor the use of the four research-based literacy practices in their classrooms.

Using what the team learned about monitoring the use of strategies, they develop strategies for each objective. The strategy for the third objective is

Monitor the use of research-based literacy practices in all classrooms by developing a system for principals to conduct weekly classroom walkthroughs.

As the team completes its identification of strategies to meet the objectives, Dr. Dunbar realizes something and comments to the group, "You know, we have tried so many ways to help students improve their achievement, but I can't remember ever knowing for sure that we've fully implemented the programs we've planned, and whether they've ever helped students in reading. Next year, we need to start collecting evidence that we've done what we said what we would do, and that our strategies have a positive effect on students.

Before we go any further, let's think about how we can collect evidence of implementation and impact."

Curriculum Director Oscar Franklin states his agreement, saying that at no time in the past does he remember ever collecting evidence on implementation and impact. He strongly recommends that the team determine how they will measure implementation and impact of each strategy before going any further in the development of the improvement plan. The team works together to determine the evidence they will collect to measure implementation and impact for each strategy and record it in their district improvement plan. To make sure they think about collecting multiple sources of data, they review Bernhardt's four measures of data.

For the third strategy—monitor the use of research-based literacy practices in all classrooms—Delightful teacher Gail Perkins suggests that principals examine weekly lesson plans for evidence that teachers are using literacy practices. Dr. Dunbar points out, however, that while lesson plans reflect what teachers intend to do, they really don't provide evidence that practices are actually being used. Furthermore, they don't show how successful teachers are in using the practices. She suggests instead that they develop procedures for principals to monitor classroom instruction and collect data related to the use of research-based literacy practices. These data will serve as evidence of implementation of the monitoring strategy.

The team then considers evidence of impact for this strategy. They decide to use data from monitoring procedures to help them determine additional support teachers need to implement research-based literacy practices.

By now the Grandville leadership team is beginning to see the potential that this plan has to help them reach their ideal state. After identifying evidence of implementation and impact for each strategy, the team turns to developing action steps for each strategy. For the strategy on monitoring the use of research-based literacy strategies, the team works together to identify three action steps.

Develop a system to analyze and report classroom walkthrough data on the implementation of research-based literacy practices.

Use the classroom walkthrough data to plan ongoing professional development.

Share data on the use of research-based literacy practices.

For each of these action steps, the team identifies the person responsible for ensuring that the action step is taken, allocates resources to implement the action step, sets a date when the action step will be completed, and establishes benchmark dates for when the action step will be monitored throughout the school year.

When the plan is completed, the district leadership team celebrates their accomplishments. While the process was a lot of hard work, they are pleased with their plan and express their commitment to following through with it. Superintendent Dunbar then provides a reality check, noting that it will take a team effort from leaders at the district, school, and classroom levels to ensure the plan is implemented. She especially stresses the importance of leaders communicating clear expectations about the improvement work being a priority and building the needed capacity to carry out the improvement plan. She also stresses the importance of frequent and regular monitoring and reviewing of the work as it progresses, and of responding quickly to needs that emerge during the implementation of the plan.

Delightful's reading coach Tonya Sykes expresses concern that after all the hard work on the plan it will be disheartening to change it in response to unanticipated events that are sure to occur in the district. Dr. Dunbar assures Ms. Sykes and the rest of the team that it will not be necessary to change the plan significantly; however, throughout the year the plan should be revised to address unanticipated needs. She suggests that a very simple revision form be used in order to document any changes.

Before adjourning this meeting, the team establishes specific dates to review progress in the implementation and impact of the plan.

Formalize and Communicate
the District Improvement Plan

Superintendent Dunbar is highly energized after working with the district leadership team on the improvement plan and wants to formally recognize the team members who worked so hard. She asks team members to take major responsibility for presenting the improvement plan to the school board at its next meeting. This is the first time a district plan has been presented to the board in this way. The team's presentation includes a description of how the plan was developed and how it will be implemented, as well as how the leadership team will need the board's support to keep the improvement effort a priority. The team members express confidence that the process used to develop the district plan will help the schools create their own improvement plans. Dr. Dunbar closes the school board meeting by urging it to provide support in terms of policies, procedures, and resources for the implementation of the district and school plans.

Team members then make plans for school representatives on the district leadership team to present the district plan to the schools. They are eager to explain how the needs and challenges of Delightful and Fairview schools were considered as the district plan was developed and to emphasize how the district intends to provide support for these schools as they address their needs. This ensures that the improvement efforts address unique needs at both the district and school level, but at the same time are mutually supportive.

Develop School Improvement Plans

After actively participating in the development of the district improvement plan, Delightful principal Mark Martinez feels confident that he can use the same process to work with his team to develop the school improvement plan. Mr. Martinez asks Gail Perkins and Tonya Sykes, Delightful's two teacher representatives to the district team, to take a lead role in guiding the school *leadership team through the process. Ms. Perkins sees this as a step forward in her professional aspirations to become a principal herself and happily agrees. Having served as an active member on the district leadership team, she works successfully with her team and is especially instrumental in developing strategies and actions in the school plan that will support the district plan. The school plan is completed by July 1, and the school leadership team determines how to share the plan with the staff on the first day of the next school year.*

Additional materials and resources related to
Getting Serious About the System can be found at
http://www.corwin.com/gettingserious

5

Phase IV

Taking Action and Monitoring Progress

Taking Action and Monitoring Progress is the fourth of five phases in the systemic approach to improvement. The first three phases focus on data analysis, review of research, and planning required for carrying out the work at the district, school, and classroom levels. In those initial phases, leaders sharpen the focus for the work ahead and develop specific strategies and timelines. By the end of the first three phases, leaders in the system will have developed and agreed on the following elements:

- The schools participating in the initial systemic effort
- District and school problem statements that summarize the central issues to be addressed
- Descriptions of the ideal state that the district and schools are working to achieve
- A district improvement plan that includes goals, objectives, strategies, action steps, resources, and a timeline
- A school improvement plan for each participating school, aligned to the district plan, that includes goals, objectives, strategies, action steps, resources, and a timeline
- A calendar of meetings for the district and school leadership teams
- Specific dates on the district and school calendars when leaders will formally monitor implementation and impact of their plans

During the first three phases of the work, the district and school leadership teams play a critical role in implementing a sequence of steps designed to move the process forward. In Phase IV, staff members carry out the planned actions at the district, school, and classroom levels. Individuals at each level have responsibilities for implementing the improvement plan. For example, district-level leaders establish procedures and allocate resources that are needed to support the plans. School leaders support the improvement work by building necessary capacity among teachers and other school staff. Teachers work collaboratively to examine data and plan instruction in order to improve student learning outcomes.

District and school leaders monitor—both formally and informally—implementation of strategies, evaluate the impact of those strategies, and review the next steps to determine whether modifications need to be made to the improvement plan. As changes are made, leaders communicate the changes throughout the system, ensure that necessary resources will be available, and build capacity to carry out the work. Staff members take action and the improvement work continues. Figure 5.1 illustrates the cyclic nature of the improvement work.

Figure 5.1 The Five Phases of Systemic Improvement Work

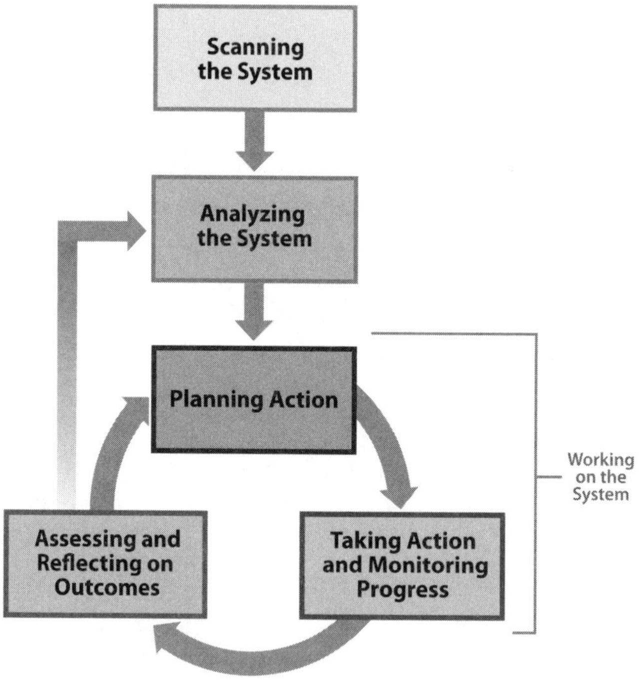

Phase IV consists of three steps, however it should be noted that they are not linear in nature. Step 1 establishes the structure that will guide the implementation process, and Steps 2 and 3 recur throughout the improvement work wherever necessary:

Step 1. Implement and Monitor the Improvement Plans. In this step, district and school leaders establish structures for meeting regularly and reviewing progress to date, planning next steps, and monitoring implementation so that they can continue to make informed decisions and adjustments over the course of the school year. This step also provides opportunities for reflection on the part of the leadership teams.

Step 2. Provide Continuing Leadership for the Improvement Work. The second step focuses on the three leadership roles necessary for implementing the plan. These roles include communicating clear expectations regarding roles and responsibilities; building capacity in the skills and knowledge needed to carry out the work, as well as providing necessary resources; and monitoring and reviewing implementation and impact data.

Step 3. Address Unique Challenges as They Arise. In the third step, district and school leaders examine data and revise improvement plans to address challenges as they arise. As changes to plans are made, leaders communicate these changes to a broad audience throughout the system to ensure that everyone is aware of their roles and responsibilities in continuing the improvement work.

Prior to this phase, district and school leaders have focused on developing improvement plans to address systemic issues contributing to problems hindering student achievement. They have also been working on the competencies necessary to sustain the improvement effort, including building strong professional relationships. As implementation begins, it is important for leaders to understand that challenges and frustrations are likely to occur, especially when individuals and groups are asked to change long-established behaviors and practices. Staff members often experience confusion and anxiety, and the strong professional relationships that are being forged will help alleviate such feelings.

Leaders may also face a challenge in maintaining focus and momentum throughout the course of the improvement process. Day-to-day distractions of running a school system often cause them to lose sight of the established goals. Leadership teams play a critical role in keeping commitment to improvement in the spotlight. Figure 5.2 shows that Phase IV helps build all the competencies involved in the systemic improvement process.

Figure 5.2 Competences Developed in Phase IV

PHASE	Competencies				
	Coherence	*Data*	*Professional Learning*	*Relationships*	*Change*
Phase IV: Taking Action and Monitoring Implementation Purpose: Establish frameworks for meeting regularly, implementing strategies, and monitoring improvement efforts	X	X	X	X	X

STEP 1. IMPLEMENT AND MONITOR THE IMPROVEMENT PLANS

In Step 1, the district and school leadership teams begin implementing their respective improvement plans. These plans map out who will carry out what actions and by when. Members of the district and school leadership teams provide encouragement, guidance, and support to those responsible for implementation throughout the improvement process.

1.1 Establish Meeting Structures for Guiding and Monitoring Implementation of the Improvement Plans

Sustaining the improvement work over time requires leaders to maintain frequent contact with the staff members carrying out the action steps. Regular meetings with those staff members are essential not only for guiding the work and gaining information about needs, but also for providing opportunities to acknowledge progress and offer encouragement and support.

Planning and actively participating in leadership team meetings and professional development communicates leaders' commitment to improvement efforts. The regular team meetings, established earlier, provide the structure and process needed to guide implementation of the improvement plan. Thoughtful and intentional planning of these meetings will significantly affect the success of the effort. Scheduling meetings on at least a monthly basis helps ensure that the improvement work remains a priority throughout the system. Regular meetings also provide opportunities to monitor the work closely and respond to changing conditions.

As emphasized earlier, it is important for leadership teams to establish and abide by a set of norms and guidelines for meetings. Teams should review information in Phase II, Step 1.2 relating to these meeting elements to integrate them into the meeting process. It is possible that norms and guidelines established earlier may require adjustments to accommodate the focus of more current meetings.

As the team begins to implement the improvement plan, the standing agenda might include the following elements:

- **The past month's actions and their subsequent results.** Team members review recently completed actions and discuss how they were implemented and what happened as a result. They discuss the challenges and successes that they experienced or observed and also reflect on circumstances and factors that led to those challenges or successes.
- **Actions in progress.** Team members report on current actions and recognize milestones reached. They also review any new data and discuss current challenges they are encountering, as well as ideas for overcoming these challenges.
- **Additional or modified support needed to maintain progress and momentum.** Leaders should consider how to provide support for the work, including providing professional learning, allocating necessary

resources, and addressing challenges as they arise. Regularly reviewing data in these areas is an effective strategy for identifying critical needs.

Building in reflection time at the end of meetings helps team members process new insights and explore how to improve meetings. This time also provides an opportunity to reinforce the primary goal of improving student achievement.

It is important for leaders to incorporate their reflections into future work with leadership teams and committee work. Some questions that may be useful are the following:

- How did our meeting go? What worked well and what didn't?
- What was the most productive part of the meeting?
- Did anything happen that got in the way of our conversation and learning?
- What new ideas or learning surfaced during the meeting?
- What actions, responsibilities, and timelines did we agree on during the meeting?
- What resources are needed to achieve the actions?
- What, if anything, should be changed in our meetings?
- What new questions do I have as a result of our meeting?

Stop and Check

Before taking the next step, make sure the following events have occurred:

✓ Members of the district and school leadership teams have established meeting structures for guiding and monitoring the implementation of the improvement plan.
✓ Members of the district and school leadership teams have identified standing agenda items to help them monitor implementation of the improvement plans.
✓ District and school leadership teams are conducting monthly meetings and are keeping the improvement plans as the focus of their attention.

STEP 2. PROVIDE CONTINUING LEADERSHIP FOR THE IMPROVEMENT WORK

2.1 Assume Responsibility for the Improvement Work

In Phase III, the leadership team reviewed three leadership roles and added action steps to the improvement plan to carry out these roles. During Phase IV, as implementation of the plan begins, it becomes crucial for leaders at every level of the local system to assume responsibility for all aspects of the improvement work. Leaders build their capacity to plan, implement, and support strategies and processes necessary to carry out the work in schools, particularly at the classroom level.

Part of the capacity building may include developing the knowledge and skills leaders need to monitor the improvement work. For example, administrators need to monitor the implementation of research-based instructional strategies. This requires regular visits to classrooms, with a defined focus for the visits. Because monitoring is crucial for successful implementation of any new initiative, if leaders do not know how to perform this function, they may need coaching in this area.

As the district and school staff begin to implement their improvement plans, they should consider key questions such as these:

- What questions do staff have about aspects of the plan and what clarifications are needed?
- What issues do leaders need to address in order to sustain progress and momentum? How should they address these issues?
- What professional learning or resource needs do staff members have? How should leaders provide for these needs?
- Are there areas in which additional support is needed? How should leaders provide this support?

The roles that are critical to maintaining momentum and keeping the improvement effort on track are the same as the ones discussed earlier, both in the **PTLC Module** and the **Leadership Module** used in Phase III. This repetition is indicative of the paramount importance of leadership in the systemic improvement process.

2.2 Communicate Clear Expectations About the Improvement Work

Keeping a long-term effort a priority for its duration can be extraordinarily difficult for leaders, especially in an environment with many competing, and sometimes conflicting, demands. The district and school leadership teams play crucial roles in keeping the goals a priority at all levels of the system. Leadership teams should detail their communication strategies and incorporate them into district and school improvement plans. Among actions that leaders take to communicate clear expectations are the following:

- **Stating explicitly that this work is and will remain a priority.** Effective leaders build this message into their communication throughout the school year—in speech, in writing, and in action. Delivering this message clearly and frequently is a powerful way leaders increase commitment of staff members and obtain results.

- **Reiterating the long-term nature of the work.** An inconsistent approach sends conflicting messages to staff members about whether or not the work is indeed a priority. They may feel that they will not truly be held responsible for implementing the improvement plan or that the work will no longer be a priority the following year.

- **Maintaining open communication with all stakeholders.** In order for the improvement work to remain systemic, individuals at all levels need to be informed of key decisions made and accomplishments achieved. They should also have multiple opportunities to provide input into decisions and to understand how these decisions will affect their work. Communicating with other important stakeholders, such as families and community groups, adds valuable perspectives and helps to broaden understanding and commitment to the improvement work.

2.3 Build Capacity to Support the Improvement Work Throughout the System

District and school leaders need to ensure that staff members develop the knowledge and skills required to implement the improvement plan. Particularly important is the ability to use data to inform decisions. The leaders regularly review implementation and impact evidence from the improvement plan(s) and collect additional data when needed. This review process, at both the district and school levels, frequently reveals the need for resources or professional learning among the instructional staff or the leaders themselves.

From time to time, leaders must make adjustments to the improvement plan(s) based on an understanding of evolving staff needs. For example, working collaboratively on the common core or state standards or district curriculum may require new knowledge and skills in instructional or assessment strategies. Building the capacity of staff to do the improvement work is a fundamental part of providing leadership and, ultimately, increasing student achievement. It may be helpful to refer to resources pertaining to professional learning on the Bibliography Matrix provided at the end of the book.

An additional consideration for building capacity is the allocation of needed resources to implement the improvement plan. These resources include the personnel to complete planned actions (e.g., content specialists), staff time (e.g., for collaboration in the PTLC), and funds needed to support the work (e.g., purchase of instructional materials). Although these elements should be specified in the improvement plan, leaders need to remain flexible in resource allocation as they respond to changing conditions. Consistently providing appropriate resources as the work evolves helps maintain momentum and communicates to staff members that their efforts are supported and valued and that this work remains a top priority.

2.4 Monitor and Review the Improvement Work

Monitoring implementation and impact of the strategies in the improvement plan is a critical part of systemic improvement. Information gained from regular and frequent reviews of the plan helps guide decisions about how best to direct the work and support the individuals responsible for implementation.

Because monitoring occurs both formally and informally, leaders need to be familiar with both approaches as methods for collecting data. Informal monitoring may occur in day-to-day conversations with the individuals carrying out the plan. This proactive approach communicates that the work is a priority and provides immediate information about challenges and issues.

Formal monitoring is more structured in nature and sometimes requires data collection tools or protocols. Leaders at the district and school levels should schedule formal reviews of the progress made to date by those individuals charged with carrying out aspects of the improvement plan. These reviews, which should occur at least quarterly, provide valuable information for decisions about adjustments to the improvement plans and timelines. In each formal review session, participants should

- review the planned actions that were scheduled to be completed by the meeting date and determine whether they were accomplished,
- identify what supported successfully completed strategies and what will help sustain the momentum, and
- identify challenges and issues that prevented successful completion of strategies and determine steps needed to accomplish these tasks.

The leadership team clarifies how to address emerging issues. Categorizing issues as follows is a helpful strategy for determining the most appropriate responses:

- Issues that leaders can easily address and handle informally without involving other individuals
- Issues that could be best handled as a function of a leader's position in the system (e.g., coaching or supervision)
- Issues that may require discussion with other district or school leaders

Monitoring implementation requires leaders to track progress so they can adjust the planned actions and accomplish goals more effectively. However, they should recognize that the term "monitoring" might carry negative connotations. Staff may perceive monitoring with concern, for example, if they believe that leaders are actually evaluating their individual performances, checking whether or not they are doing their jobs, or investigating concerns about the abilities of individual staff members. These misconceptions may contribute to a culture of distrust and ultimately reduce the overall effectiveness of the improvement effort. Communication to staff members about monitoring in a positive sense, especially early in the work, should include the following four points:

- Defining that monitoring of the plan is a means of checking progress, not evaluating individuals
- Explaining how and why monitoring plays a critical role in implementing an improvement plan
- Emphasizing how monitoring implementation of the plan is different from evaluating the performance of individuals (each of these tasks is done for distinctly different purposes and in different ways)
- Detailing why and how monitoring will occur, particularly at the classroom level

Stop and Check

Before taking the next step, make sure the following events have occurred:

✓ District and school leaders are assuming responsibility for the improvement work.

✓ District and school leadership teams are implementing strategies for communicating clear expectations as specified in their improvement plans.

✓ District and school leadership teams are implementing strategies for building capacity as specified in their improvement plans.

✓ District and school leadership teams are implementing strategies for monitoring and reviewing as specified in their improvement plans.

STEP 3. ADDRESS UNIQUE CHALLENGES AS THEY ARISE

3.1 Analyze Data Collected Through the Monitoring Process

Every school system is unique. A distinctive combination of factors influences how educational stakeholders perceive, describe, and implement an improvement effort. Challenges and needs that are specific to a particular system emerge as the work unfolds. For example, perhaps adequate resources such as staff or budget allotments have not been allocated to implement one or more action steps. Or an unexpected turnover in key leadership positions has created a vacuum in the driving force behind the improvement work. To address the challenges that arise, leadership teams need to examine the research related to best practices about the issues. Anticipating challenges before they occur and addressing emergent issues in a timely manner helps ensure that the work continues to move forward and that implementation remains the central focus for leaders. Using research at every step of the improvement process should become part of the culture of the system.

The leaders continue to analyze and summarize information collected through the monitoring process in order to make informed decisions about next steps and future planning. They examine the evidence of implementation and impact as specified in their improvement plans. They also discuss what they have observed or heard while informally monitoring implementation of individual strategies. These data provide extremely useful feedback concerning the extent to which strategies are being carried out, whether they are having the desired outcomes, and whether unanticipated issues have emerged.

As district and school leaders review their data, they reflect on their findings and how these findings may affect their improvement plans. If this examination reveals that strategies are not being carried out as intended or they are not moving the district and schools toward the ideal state, then the teams should consider revising their plans or timelines. Unanticipated issues that need to be addressed may be included in the updated plans.

3.2 Update the Plans and Communicate Changes

Leaders update the district and campus improvement plans based on their data reviews. Adjustments may include revising existing strategies; adding or deleting action steps; or adjusting the timeline, responsibilities, resources, or evidence of implementation or impact. Figure 5.3, the Improvement Plan Revision Form, is designed to help leaders track and document changes made to the improvement plan. (A full-sized version of the form is available in the Strategies and Action Steps Module handouts, found on the companion website.)

Changes to the district improvement plan need to be communicated to the participating schools because these changes may necessitate adjustments to the school improvement plans. Any significant changes to district and school plans should be communicated throughout the system.

Figure 5.3 Improvement Plan Revision Form

Revisions to Plan and/or Next Steps				
After review of actions at set benchmark timelines, what are the revisions we will make if the initial plan is not working or if additional steps are needed?				
Goal #, Objective #, Strategy #: (Strategy text)				
Action Steps	**Person(s) Responsible**	**Resources**	**Completion Date**	**Benchmark Timeline**
(Identify action step # that needs to be revised and the revised step. Add steps as needed.)				

Stop and Check

Before taking the next step, make sure the following events have occurred:

✓ District and school leaders are collecting and analyzing data on an ongoing basis to monitor implementation and impact of the improvement plans.

✓ District and school leaders are updating their improvement plans based on their data reviews.

✓ District and school leaders are communicating revisions to the plans to schools and other stakeholders, as appropriate.

Phase IV at Grandville School District and Delightful Intermediate School

Implement and Monitor Improvement Plans

At the beginning of the school year, due to staff turnover, it becomes necessary for the Grandville district leadership team to replace two of its members. Dr. Dunbar orients the new members to their roles, meeting norms, and operating guidelines. At the first meeting of the district leadership team, members review the improvement plan, their roles and responsibilities, and evidence they will collect to determine implementation and impact.

As Grandville District and Delightful Intermediate School begin to implement their plans, they confirm their previously established structures for meeting regularly and reviewing progress in order to make informed decisions and adjustments over the course of the school year.

At Delightful School, Mark Martinez schedules time to review the school improvement plan with all staff as well as parents and community members. The members of the school leadership team describe how the plan was developed, including the data that indicated needs to be addressed. They also share how the plan will be implemented and monitored and how they will keep the improvement effort a priority at the school.

As the Delightful leadership team begins to oversee the implementation of their plan, Mr. Martinez continues to emphasize the importance of collaboration and a professional culture that reflects trust and respect. At each meeting of the team, they monitor the past month's actions and analyze the results they are seeing. This ongoing process of monitoring and reviewing reveals that teachers need more intensive assistance in implementing one of the new literacy practices.

Provide Leadership for the Improvement Work

Throughout this process, the importance of strong and effective leadership becomes clearer to members of Delightful's team. They realize that consistent communication, in both written and verbal form, is critically important to keeping the staff focused on the improvement effort and the district informed of the school's progress and needs. They also determine that they will need to support the staff as they learn to use the four new literacy practices throughout the school year. They plan to do this through a variety of ways, including workshops, coaching, and collaborative interactions. Monitoring implementation of the practices, by means of classroom walkthroughs and visits to PTLC meetings, provides valuable information about the extent to which the new literacy practices are being implemented and which teachers would benefit from additional support.

Address Unique Challenges as They Arise

Based on their ongoing review of implementation and impact data, Mr. Martinez and the Delightful team determine that teachers who are struggling with the literacy practices will need additional opportunities for professional learning. They decide that Ms. Sykes, the school's reading coach, will model use of the practices in classrooms followed by reflective debriefing with teachers. The team updates the school improvement plan to reflect this additional support. They share the data that informed this decision and the details about how the new action step will be implemented and monitored.

Mr. Martinez includes this update in his monthly report to the district leadership team as specified in the district's plan to monitor and support the progress of schools.

Additional materials and resources related to
Getting Serious About the System can be found at
http://www.corwin.com/gettingserious

6

Phase V

Assessing and Reflecting on Outcomes

Assessing and Reflecting on Outcomes is the fifth of the five phases in the systemic improvement approach. During Phase IV, leaders implemented and monitored their improvement plans at both the district and school levels. As they did so, they demonstrated three essential leadership roles: communicating clear expectations, building capacity, and monitoring and reviewing. Leaders also addressed unique challenges that arose and updated their improvement plans based on these challenges, as well as their examination of implementation and impact data.

Throughout all previous phases, the leaders will have evaluated and reflected on their improvement work. In Phase V, however, leaders consider the overall effectiveness of their planned strategies and actions, as evidenced by year-end student performance data and other impact data. As a result, the evaluation and reflection in this final phase becomes much more summative in nature.

Although this is the last of the five phases in the systemic approach to improvement, it does not represent an end to the improvement work because the process is cyclical in nature. In Phase V, leaders determine the focus of the continuing work. It is also a time for an important, and sometimes neglected, element of the improvement process: celebration of accomplishments.

Phase V consists of three steps:

Step 1. Analyze and Reflect on Evidence of Implementation and Impact. Throughout the previous phase, Taking Action and Monitoring Progress, school and district leaders collected and analyzed data on the implementation and impact of the improvement effort. Now they summarize these data to guide discussions and decisions about the focus for continuing the work.

Step 2. Decide on a Focus for Continuing the Improvement Work. Based on their discussions and review of the data, the district and school leadership teams identify next steps and develop specific strategies for communicating decisions on their continuing improvement efforts.

Step 3. Recognize Work, Progress, and Accomplishments. Leaders recognize and celebrate the accomplishments of staff members at all levels in their efforts to increase student achievement.

Figure 6.1 shows the competencies that are focused on in Phase V.

Figure 6.1 Competencies Developed in Phase V

PHASE	Competencies				
	Coherence	Data	Professional Learning	Relationships	Change
Phase V: Assessing and Reflecting on Outcomes Purpose: Determine to what degree the improvement plan is being implemented and monitored; analyze actions in relation to intended outcomes	X	X		X	

STEP 1. ANALYZE AND REFLECT ON EVIDENCE OF IMPLEMENTATION AND IMPACT

1.1 Analyze Evidence of Implementation and Impact in Participating Schools

In order to evaluate progress on a systemwide basis, the district leadership team needs information from each of the participating schools about their accomplishments and challenges in reaching their own and the district's ideal state. Because outcomes are typically framed in terms of increased student achievement, it is best to initiate the review process as soon as year-end achievement results are available.

The district team directs each school leadership team to analyze data and prepare a summary report. A comparison of student achievement data in content areas before and after implementation of the improvement plan should be included in this report. Implementation and impact data specified in the school improvement plan (including any revisions made on the Improvement Plan Revision Form) should also be a major focus of this report. Other sources of data may include

- the Rubric for Determining System Capacity;
- formal and informal assessments of student progress not included in the improvement plan;

- summaries of classroom walkthrough data;
- one or more sections of the System Examination Tool;
- meeting agendas and notes from school leadership team meetings; and
- the discussions, input, and decisions that took place over the course of the school year among school leadership team members and among school staff.

Before examining these data, school leaders revisit federal, state, and local goals for student learning and review how to interpret the various data reports, if necessary. Working in small groups, the team compares their student learning outcomes to these goals in order to identify, discuss, and chart important information that "pops out" (using the process described in the **Pop-Outs Module** in Phase II). This process is repeated for each accumulated data set. The team then looks across the charts to find consistencies, inconsistencies, and other interesting information from their data. They reflect on their findings to identify continuing or emerging systemic issues that need to be addressed in the ongoing improvement work.

Using the Summative Analysis and Reflection Guide (Figure 6.2) to stimulate discussion, the school team draws upon the gathered information to create the report requested by the district team. In their report, the school leaders provide an overall summary of the extent to which they implemented the work as planned and whether it had the desired impact. They also describe their efforts related to each objective. Findings should be supported with specific evidence and examples so that district leaders can see how conclusions were drawn. The

Figure 6.2 Summative Analysis and Reflection Guide

Implementation

1. In this current school year, to what extent have staff members effectively carried out their assignments related to the improvement effort as planned?

2. In what ways have leaders effectively monitored the work done and provided timely direction and support to the staff members carrying out the improvement work at all levels of the system?

3. What challenges or difficulties did leaders and teachers encounter while implementing the improvement plan and monitoring implementation?

4. What successes or accomplishments did staff members experience while implementing the improvement plan and monitoring implementation?

5. What are the insights that leaders have gained this year about implementing and monitoring the improvement plan, and how can they be used when planning for the coming year?

Impact

6. How has the implementation of the improvement plan achieved the intended outcomes as defined by the campus leadership team in the plan?

7. What changes in student achievement scores have occurred since the beginning of the improvement work?

8. What changes have occurred in the daily work at the district, school, and classroom levels that support the alignment of curriculum, instruction, and assessment to the state standards?

report should strike a balance between highlighting successes and identifying challenges that the school will need to overcome as the work continues.

It is important for district leaders to communicate that the report is not intended to evaluate whether or not the school "passed or failed." Rather, the purpose of this document is to provide a starting point for a conversation among school and district leaders about the progress of the system as a whole in reaching the ideal state.

1.2 Analyze Evidence of Implementation and Impact Systemwide

Members of the district leadership team begin their formal assessment and reflection by determining to what degree the district and school improvement plans have been implemented and monitored with fidelity. Analyzing summative results will reveal how the overall system is progressing and whether the current effort is on track for achieving the ultimate goal of increasing student performance. The analysis will have implications for the future direction of the work. This progress review should focus on the following questions:

1. Did the district and schools do what they set out to do? (Implementation)

2. Did the strategies used at the district and school levels make a difference in teaching and learning? (Impact)

The district team replicates the process used at the school level for analyzing data, including revisiting federal, state, and local goals for student learning and identifying trends and other information that "pop out" of various data sets. The team consolidates data on the level of implementation and impact contained in the reports from each of the participating schools. Team members compare student learning data in the content areas before and after implementation of the improvement plan at each of the schools. They also compare the performance level of students in participating schools to those in other schools in the district and to overall district results.

Implementation and impact data specified in the district improvement plan (including any revisions made on the Improvement Plan Revision Form, in Phase IV) should also be a major focus of this analysis. Other sources of data, in addition to the report submitted by each school, may include

- the Rubric for Determining System Capacity;
- formal and informal assessments of student progress not included in the improvement plan;
- survey results (e.g., of professional development needs, school culture, family and community involvement);
- one or more sections of the System Examination Tool;
- meeting agendas and notes from district leadership team meetings; and
- the discussions, input, and decisions that took place over the course of the school year among district leadership team members and among district staff.

Members of the district leadership team collaboratively analyze and reflect on the progress and challenges encountered at both the district and school levels. This analysis helps identify key issues and sets the stage for discussions about the starting point and direction of the work in the coming year. The Summative Analysis and Reflection Guide can help organize this process. Specific evidence and examples should be cited to support conclusions. This information will be used to communicate progress and future plans to internal and external stakeholders in Step 2.2 of this phase.

Stop and Check

Before taking the next step, make sure the following events have occurred:

✓ District leaders have guided school leaders in analyzing and reporting on the evidence of implementation and impact of their improvement plans.
✓ District leaders have analyzed evidence of implementation and impact systemwide.

STEP 2. DECIDE ON A FOCUS FOR CONTINUING THE IMPROVEMENT WORK

2.1 Determine Next Steps for Continuing the Improvement Work

The next steps for continuing the work in the coming year are determined by issues that emerged from the data analysis and reflection process just completed. The district leadership team reviews the progress that has been made to date and considers the extent to which the problem statements have been addressed. They review the Summative Analysis and Reflection Guide and then examine whether the issues just identified are addressed in the existing improvement plans.

For issues that are addressed in the plans, the team members must decide whether there have been substantial problems with implementation of the relevant strategies and action steps. They also examine whether the action steps, if carried out, were effective in implementing the strategy.

If action steps were *not* carried out as intended, the team will need to discuss why this happened and what should be done to ensure future implementation. They may decide to (1) establish a stronger commitment to the improvement work or (2) adjust the scope and/or timeline of the improvement plan so it can be accomplished. The discussion may reveal that an action step was not implemented for the simple reason that it was not appropriate or that resources were not available to support implementation.

Should leaders decide to make considerable revisions to the scope of the improvement plan, they need to ensure that the work remains focused on achieving the ideal state as a means to increase student learning. The revised plan must remain substantial enough to have a significant impact on achieving this goal.

If leaders determine that the improvement plan *was* implemented and monitored with fidelity, they analyze whether the strategies had their intended results. If the desired impact was achieved, the team will want to consider how to ensure sustainability of the improved system, as well as how to recognize success.

However, if the intended *impact* was *not* realized, leaders may need to give their current work more time or devote additional resources to be effective. Leaders should keep in mind that large-scale systemic change is accomplished incrementally and that student achievement gains may not occur in the first year of implementation as new processes are introduced and capacity is built (Jenlink, Reigeluth, Carr, & Nelson, 1998; Murphy & Meyers, 2008).

In some cases, the analysis may reveal that the action steps or resources were inadequate for achieving intended outcomes. This finding will require leaders to examine the research and reconsider their action steps and available resources. Additional or more effective steps may need to be included in the revised improvement plan for the coming year. Leaders follow a similar procedure in determining how effective the strategies were in achieving their objectives and how effective the objectives were in reaching the goal.

It is quite likely that improvement efforts to achieve the ideal state will require more than one year of planning and implementation. Some schools in the system may need more time and assistance to achieve their goals and objectives. In such instances, the district will determine additional support and pressure, if necessary, required by those schools.

At the same time, other schools that have had successful results may be ready to move forward, and the district must support these schools in their continued improvement efforts as well. The decision of whether to expand or intensify the current work or to shift the focus area (e.g., from curriculum to instruction) will have to be based on the needs of schools in both of the situations described earlier.

When leaders agree that the current focus area is successful and sustainable, team members should consider expanding the current work by shifting to a new focus area, as mentioned previously, or moving to a new content area (e.g., from mathematics to reading). In either case, they will cycle back to an earlier phase of the systemic improvement approach. This usually occurs as leaders and staff become comfortable with the approach, observe its positive impact firsthand, and gain more experience coordinating their efforts. Leaders should have a clear understanding of the sequence of phases and steps in order to select the specific point in the systemic approach that would be most appropriate for beginning the work in the next school year.

However, leaders should remember that once they have achieved success in a certain area, they cannot assume that it no longer requires attention. Areas of success need ongoing oversight and support to ensure that effective strategies become standard ways of working and to maintain momentum for continuous improvement.

2.2 Develop Specific Strategies for Informing Stakeholders of Accomplishments and Decisions

The district leadership team needs to communicate to the leaders in each of the participating schools, as well as to other stakeholders, the accomplishments and decisions made at this stage of the work. Team members outline a strategy for communicating their decisions regarding continuation of the systemic improvement work to school leaders, the school board, parents, and the local community. Sharing information of this nature fosters continuing support for cohesive and coherent improvement efforts and strengthens relationships that have been established.

2.3 Ensure That the School Leaders Have a Clear Understanding of the Focus for the Continuing Improvement Work

District team members ensure that school teams have a clear understanding of progress made, challenges that remain, and the district focus for the coming year. Representatives from the district team help school leaders understand the implications of the revised district plan for the school and classroom levels in order to refine their school improvement plans.

District leaders assist the school teams in determining next steps for their improvement work, using the Summative Analysis and Reflection Guide completed by the schools in Step 1.1. The data on implementation and impact at the school level will inform decisions on whether to revise the current action steps, expand current efforts, or perhaps focus on a new content area. It is important that the revised school improvement plans remain aligned to the district plan and that the plans continue to be mutually supportive.

Stop and Check

Before taking the next step, make sure the following events have occurred:

✓ The district leadership team has determined next steps for continuing the improvement work.

✓ The district leadership team has developed a strategy for informing stakeholders of accomplishments and decisions on the continuing work.

✓ The district leadership team has ensured that schools leaders have a clear understanding of the district focus for the continuing improvement work.

✓ The district leadership team has guided leaders at each participating school in determining next steps.

STEP 3. RECOGNIZE WORK, PROGRESS, AND ACCOMPLISHMENTS

3.1 Summarize the Accomplishments to Date and the Progress Made Toward Achieving the Ideal State

Taking time to recognize the efforts, achievements, and successes of teachers and leaders is an important aspect of promoting long-term success in systemic improvement. Staff members develop a greater sense of ownership and are more likely to embrace the overall effort when they are acknowledged for their contributions and see real progress toward improving student learning as a result of their work. Leaders should make a conscious effort to identify and celebrate the contributions made by staff members at all levels of the system. The informal recognition of staff involvement is an integral part of the monitoring that occurs throughout the improvement work, whenever and wherever it happens. However, at this point, leaders recognize more formally the contributions of staff as a whole in reaching this milestone.

Leaders at the district and school levels may use the Summative Analysis and Reflection Guide to summarize accomplishments and progress made to date. The leaders can then clearly articulate how each accomplishment advances the system toward its ideal state.

3.2 Develop and Implement Strategies for Recognizing Accomplishments and Celebrating Success

Once leaders have identified district- and school-level accomplishments, they determine the specific strategies they will use to recognize staff members for their efforts, perseverance, and contributions toward goals. This recognition of efforts helps to establish a community of individuals who feel supported and are motivated to persist through the hard work of sustained improvement.

The precise nature of this recognition may vary from school to school, and leaders at each school need to be aware of the attitudes and feelings of their staff in order to identify what type of recognition is most meaningful for them. For example, in one school, an informal celebration, such as an ice cream social, may be appropriate. In another school, a more formal presentation by the principal and teacher leaders at a faculty meeting or at a school board meeting may work best. Understanding the district and school cultures helps leaders make the best decisions for recognizing accomplishments. Figure 6.3 provides some examples of strategies for recognizing and celebrating progress and success.

Figure 6.3 Ideas for Celebrating Success

Ask

Every time a leader meets with a staff member, a simple technique to celebrate success is to ask what went well since the last time they met. Probe for even small examples of things that went well. Teachers may take their achievements for granted. As with many people, they may dismiss the things at which they excel because those activities seem easy to them and, thus, they are not worth mentioning. By asking, leaders are modeling that they value success at all levels and that everyone should be comfortable talking about their successes, including students and parents.

Acknowledge

Sincere recognition goes a long way in maintaining and renewing commitment to the school and the improvement effort. Take time to acknowledge efforts personally by sending a handwritten note to an individual's home or sending an eCard. These are great ways to recognize someone's accomplishments and brighten his or her day without the expense of a gift. Mention accomplishments in e-mails, bulletins, or newsletters for the school. You might provide a thank you for

- a job well done,
- outstanding service to others,
- handling a difficult situation, or
- spending time beyond what is expected.

Extend congratulations on

- recent accomplishments,
- achieving program objectives, and
- students' success.

Start a "Wall of Fame" or "Dream Team" portfolio in the office. Hang photos, names, and achievements on the wall. These can also become a scrapbook of achievements.

Articulate

When milestones are reached, celebrate by publicly promoting the success. Some ways to do this include the following:

- Treating everyone to an old fashioned cake and ice cream celebration
- Placing a big banner on your building
- Publicizing it in the local newspaper or on the district website
- Creating a "Look what's happened since we first started" scrapbook. Take photographs and keep a record of milestones, staff achievements, and group results
- Hosting a celebration party, inviting participants and their guests so that the group has a chance to celebrate their success with friends and loved ones

Vignette

PHASE V AT GRANDVILLE SCHOOL DISTRICT AND DELIGHTFUL INTERMEDIATE SCHOOL

Analyze and Reflect on Evidence of Implementation and Impact

The end of the school year provides an opportunity for both the Grandville District and Delightful School leadership teams to consider the overall effectiveness of their improvement plans and progress they have made in addressing identified needs. The teams analyze summative data that provide evidence of whether their plans were effective or not.

In examining their student achievement data, they notice that scores in reading have increased to some extent for all student groups. In fact, Delightful's reading scores reflect the greatest increase compared to other schools in the district. From their summative walk-through data, they are pleased to see increasing use of the four research-based reading practices in classrooms across the district.

Mr. Martinez leads Delightful's leadership team through a summative analysis of progress. From the data examined, it becomes apparent that the staff's hard work has paid off. The team gains great satisfaction in noting that, when compared to other Grandville schools, Delightful's reading scores show the greatest increase. The school leadership team realizes that the improvement plan has been instrumental in keeping them focused on accomplishing the work that needed to be done throughout the year. The district's and school's review of implementation and impact data lays the groundwork for next year's improvement plans.

Decide on a Focus for Continuing the Improvement Work

The district team is so pleased with the progress they have made that they are tempted to move their focus from reading to mathematics. After a lengthy discussion, however, the team decides that a shift in focus at this early stage would be premature as there is still significant work to be accomplished in the implementation of research-based reading strategies. Assuming that next year's improvement effort stays on track and produces desired outcomes, they anticipate that the district and school will be ready for a focus on mathematics at the end of the next school year.

Using the Summative Analysis and Reflection Guide, the district leadership team is able to determine that they should continue their efforts to support the use of the four original research-based reading strategies and begin implementation of four additional reading strategies in the coming year. Based on the success of the reading coach assistance to Delightful, they decide to hire an additional reading coach. This reading coach would have primary responsibility for assisting teachers at another school they decide to add to Grandville's systemic improvement effort in the coming year.

At Delightful, the team agrees that continuing the focus on reading will help sustain their improvements. The team agrees that while parent involvement has increased somewhat in the past school year, the staff needs to explore additional ways to engage family and community members in efforts that more directly support student reading performance.

Recognize Work, Progress, and Accomplishments

Superintendent Dunbar meets with the district leadership team to acknowledge formally how far the team has come in terms of working together productively, understanding and using data, and planning for improvement. Team members make plans to report their progress to the school board and recognize the accomplishments of staff members throughout the district. They also plan to invite all staff to a spaghetti dinner to celebrate successes.

At Delightful, Mr. Martinez acknowledges the staff's hard work that has resulted in the increase in reading performance. He especially recognizes the work of the school leadership team in maintaining the focus on the improvement work throughout the year. He notes that the plan has helped the staff stay on track, use resources where they are most needed, and address unanticipated challenges. The leadership team plans to host an ice cream social during the last week of school. During the social, staff will be invited to help create a banner recognizing their accomplishments. To motivate continued progress toward their goals in the coming year, this banner will be placed in the front entrance of the school.

Additional materials and resources related to
Getting Serious About the System can be found at
http://www.corwin.com/gettingserious

Continuing the Improvement Work

There is no real end to the improvement work in educational systems that have established high learning goals for students. Such organizations are continuously striving to get better at what they do. As described in Phase V, *Getting Serious About the System* offers a recursive process that allows leadership teams to decide whether to focus on another aspect of the same problem they have been addressing (e.g., enhancing family and community involvement as they continue their current concentration on effective literacy instructional strategies).

On the other hand, they may decide that systems are sufficiently in place to allow them to focus on another problem area entirely (e.g., mathematics assessment strategies). If the decision is the latter, the team would return to the gap analysis process to identify differences between practices in their newly selected focus area in their own district and schools and those of high-performing systems.

In either case, the decision on where to focus ongoing improvement efforts is based on data, research-based strategies, and multiple opportunities for collaboration and discussion. Most districts and schools find that the phases of the work can be accelerated significantly as systemic competencies among the staff are strengthened and effective practices become entrenched in the local system.

This book and its related online resources serve as a guide, or fieldbook, for district and school facilitators who want to improve learning outcomes for students. However, it is not intended as a lockstep approach. Because each system is unique, the process will, no doubt, need to be adapted from time to time to provide some degree of flexibility on the part of everyone involved. *Getting Serious About the System* simply requires us to understand what systemic improvement is, and then get started. When will you begin?

Bibliography Matrix

With References to Systemic Improvement Components

This matrix was developed to assist facilitators and leadership team members in accessing resources related to one or more of the Working Systemically components. While it is not a comprehensive list, it can be useful to those wanting to access information from reputable sources and share it with others.

Resource	Standards	Curriculum	Instruction	Assessment	Resources	Professional Staff	Policy and Governance	Family and Community
Ainsworth, L. (2004). *"Unwrapping" the standards: A simple process to make standards manageable*. Denver, CO: Advanced Learning Press.	★	★	★			★		
Aladjem, D. K., Birman, B. F., Harr-Robins, J., & Parrish, T. B. (2010). *Achieving dramatic school improvement: An exploratory study*. Washington, DC: U.S. Department of Education, Office of Planning, Evaluation and Policy Development, Policy and Program Studies Service.		★	★		★	★		
Alliance for Excellent Education. (2008, February). *What keeps good teachers in the classroom: Understanding and reducing teacher turnover* (Issue brief). Washington, DC: Author. Retrieved from http://www.all4ed.org/files/TeachTurn.pdf			★			★	★	

(Continued)

Resource	Standards	Curriculum	Instruction	Assessment	Resources	Professional Staff	Policy and Governance	Family and Community
Alliance for Excellent Education. (2008, March). *Measuring and improving the effectiveness of high school teachers* (Issue brief). Washington, DC: Author. Retrieved from http://www.all4ed.org/files/TeacherEffectiveness.pdf			★	★		★	★	
Armstrong, A. (2011, Winter). Four key strategies help educators overcome resistance to change. *Tools for Schools, 14*(2). Oxford, OH: Learning Forward.						★		
Armstrong, A. (2011, Summer). Lesson study puts a collaborative lens on student learning. *Tools for Schools, 14*(4). Oxford, OH: Learning Forward.			★			★		
Auerbach, S. (2011). Learning from Latino families. *Educational Leadership, 68*(8), 16–21.								★
Barth, R. (2006). Improving relationships within the schoolhouse. *Educational Leadership, 63*(3), 8–13.		★	★	★		★		
Barton, P. E., & Coley, R. J. (2009). Measuring the achievement elephant. *Educational Leadership, 66*(4), 30–34.				★				
Bella, N. J. (2004). *Reflective analysis of student work: Improving teaching through collaboration.* Thousand Oaks, CA: Corwin.			★	★		★		

Resource	Standards	Curriculum	Instruction	Assessment	Resources	Professional Staff	Policy and Governance	Family and Community
Bernhardt, V. L. (2004). *Data analysis for comprehensive schoolwide improvement* (2nd ed.). Larchmont, NY: Eye on Education.			★	★		★	★	★
Bernhardt, V. L. (2006). *Using data to improve student learning in school districts.* Larchmont, NY: Eye on Education.			★	★		★	★	★
Bernhardt, V. L. (2009). *Data, data everywhere.* Larchmont, NY: Eye on Education.			★	★		★	★	★
Berry, B. (2005). Recruiting and retaining board-certified teachers for hard-to-staff schools. *Phi Delta Kappan, 87*(4), 290–297.			★			★	★	
Blank, M. J., Berg, A. C., & Melaville, A. (2006). *Growing community schools: The role of cross-boundary leadership.* Washington, DC: Coalition for Community Schools. Retrieved from www.community schools.org						★	★	★
Boethel, M. (2004). *Readiness: School, family, & community connections.* Austin, TX: SEDL. Retrieved from www.sedl .org/connections/resources/ readinesssynthesis.pdf					★	★		★
Bottoms, G., & Fry, B. (2009). *The district leadership challenge: Empowering principals to improve teaching and learning.* Atlanta, GA: SREB.	★	★	★	★	★	★		★

(Continued)

Resource	Standards	Curriculum	Instruction	Assessment	Resources	Professional Staff	Policy and Governance	Family and Community
Bottoms, G., & Schmidt-Davis, J. (2010). *The three essentials: Improving schools requires district vision, district and state support, and principal leadership.* Atlanta, GA: SREB.	★	★	★	★	★	★	★	★
Boyd, D., Grossman, P., Lankford, H., Loeb, S., & Wyckoff, J. (2007). *Who leaves? Teacher attrition and student achievement.* Albany, NY: Teacher Policy Research. Retrieved from http://www.urban.org/publications/1001270.html			★			★	★	
Brin, D., Kowal, J., & Hassell, B. C. (2008). *School turnarounds: Actions and results.* Lincoln, IL: Center on Innovation and Improvement. Retrieved from http://www.centerii.org/						★	★	★
Bryk, A., & Schneider, B. (2003). Trust in schools: A core resource for school reform. *Educational Leadership, 60*(3), 40–45.						★		
Buczynski, S., & Hansen, C. B. (2010). Impact of professional development on teacher practice: Uncovering connections. *Teaching and Teacher Education, 26*(3), 599–607.		★	★	★	★	★	★	
Camburn, E. M. (2010). Embedded teacher learning opportunities as a site for reflective practice: An exploratory study. *American Journal of Education, 116*(4), 463–489.						★		

Resource	Standards	Curriculum	Instruction	Assessment	Resources	Professional Staff	Policy and Governance	Family and Community
Caspe, M., & Lopez, M. E. (2006). *Lessons from family-strengthening interventions: Learning from evidence-based practice.* Cambridge, MA: Harvard Family Research Project. Retrieved from http://www.hfrp.org/ publications-resources/ browse-our-publications/ lessons-from-family -strengthening-interven tions-learning-from-evidence -based-practice								★
Cawelti, G. (Ed.). (2004). *Handbook of research on improving student achievement* (3rd ed.). Arlington, VA: Educational Research Service.	★	★	★	★		★	★	
Cawelti, G., & Protheroe, N. (2007). The school board and central office in school improvement. In H. J. Walberg (Ed.), *Handbook on restructuring and substantial school improvement* (pp. 37–52). Lincoln, IL: Center on Innovation and Improvement. Retrieved from www.centerii.org	★	★	★		★	★	★	★
Center for Comprehensive School Reform and Improvement. (2009, September). *District support of school improvement: Highlights from three districts.* (CCSRI Newsletter). Washington, DC: Author. Retrieved from http:// www.centerforcsri.org/index. php?option=com_content&tas k=blogsection&id=3&Itemid=5		★	★		★	★	★	

(Continued)

Resource	Standards	Curriculum	Instruction	Assessment	Resources	Professional Staff	Policy and Governance	Family and Community
Center for Comprehensive School Reform and Improvement Newsletter. (2009, August). *Voices from the field: How school boards can support districtwide improvement efforts.* Washington, DC: Author. Retrieved from http://www .centerforcsri.org/index .php?option=com_content& task=blogsection&id=3&Ite mid=5						★	★	
Chenowith, K. (2007). *It's being done: Academic success in unexpected schools.* Cambridge, MA: Harvard Education Press.	★	★	★	★			★	
Childress, S., Elmore, R. F., Grossman, A. S., & Johnson, S. M. (2007). Creating coherence in district administration. *Harvard Education Letter, 23*(6), 6–8.						★	★	
Cicchinelli, L., Dean, C., Galvin, M., Goodwin, B., & Parsley, D. (2006). *Success in sight: A comprehensive approach to school improvement.* Denver, CO: Mid-continent Research for Education and Learning (McREL).		★	★	★		★	★	★
Cohen, J., McCabe, L., Mitchell, N. M., & Pickeral, T. (2009). School climate: Research, policy, practice, and teacher education. *Teachers College Record, 111*(1), 180–213.						★	★	

Resource	Standards	Curriculum	Instruction	Assessment	Resources	Professional Staff	Policy and Governance	Family and Community
Cohen, P. L., Duhon, C., Flaherty, T. D., Fryer, L., Gil, L. S., Harris, et al. (2011, January). *Eight elements of high school improvement: A mapping framework*. Washington, DC: National High School Center.	★	★	★	★	★	★	★	★
Coldren, A. F., & Spillane, J. P. (2007). Making connections to teaching practice: The role of boundary practices in instructional leadership. *Educational Policy, 21*(2), 369–396.		★	★	★		★	★	
Corallo, C., & McDonald, D. (2001). *What works with low-performing schools: A review of research literature on low-performing schools*. Charleston, WV: AEL.		★	★	★		★	★	
Cortese, A., & Zastrow, C. (2006). Closing the staffing gap and ensuring effective teaching for the students who need it most. *Education Week, 25*(19), 34–35. Retrieved from http://www.learningfirst .org/news/edweekarticl/index .html			★			★	★	
Cowan, D., Joyner, S., & Beckwith, S. (2008). *Working systemically in action: A guide for facilitators*. Austin, TX: SEDL.	★	★	★	★	★	★	★	★
Cowan, D. F. (2006). Creating learning communities in low-performing sites: A systemic approach to alignment. *Journal of School Leadership, 16*(5), 596–610.	★	★	★	★		★	★	

(Continued)

Resource	Standards	Curriculum	Instruction	Assessment	Resources	Professional Staff	Policy and Governance	Family and Community
Croft, A., Coggshall, J. G., Dolan, M., & Powers, E. (2010). *Job-embedded professional development: What it is, who is responsible, and how to get it done well* (Issue brief). Washington, DC: National Comprehensive Center for Teacher Quality.						★	★	
Crow, T. (2009, November). Lock in the power of collaboration. *The Learning System, 5*(3), 1, 4–7.			★			★		
Darling-Hammond, L., Wei, R. C., & Adamson, F. (2010). *Professional learning in the United States: Trends and challenges* (Part II of a three-Phase study), Executive summary. Dallas, TX: National Staff Development Council.						★	★	
Datnow, A., Lasky, S. G., Stringfield, S. C., & Teddlie, C. (2005). Systemic integration for educational reform in racially and linguistically diverse contexts: A summary of the evidence. *Journal of Education for Students Placed At Risk, 10*(4), 445–453.			★	★		★	★	
Datnow, A., Park, V., & Wohlstetter, P. (2007). *Achieving with data: How high-performing school systems use data to improve instruction for elementary students.* Los Angeles: University of Southern California, Center on Educational Governance.				★	★	★		

Resource	Standards	Curriculum	Instruction	Assessment	Resources	Professional Staff	Policy and Governance	Family and Community
Day, C., & Gu, Q. (2007). Variations in the conditions for teachers' professional learning and development: Sustaining commitment and effectiveness over a career. *Oxford Review of Education, 33*(4), 423–443.						★	★	
Dearing, E., Kreider, H., Simpkins, S., & Weiss, H. (2007). *Family involvement in school and low-income children's literacy performance* (Research Digest). Cambridge, MA: Harvard Family Research Project. Retrieved from http://www.hfrp.org/ family-involvement/ publications-resources/ family-involvement-in-school -and-low-income-children-s -literacy-performance								★
Delehant, A. M., & von Frank, V. (2007). *Making meetings work.* Thousand Oaks, CA: Corwin.						★	★	
Dervarics, C., & O'Brien, E. (2011, January). *Eight characteristics of effective school boards.* Alexandria, VA: Center for Public Education. Retrieved from http://www .centerforpubliceducation .org/Main-Menu/ Public-education/Eight -characteristics-of-effective -school-boards/default.aspx					★	★	★	★

(*Continued*)

Resource	Standards	Curriculum	Instruction	Assessment	Resources	Professional Staff	Policy and Governance	Family and Community
Diaz-Maggioli, G. H. (2004). *A passion for learning: Teacher-centered professional development*. Alexandria, VA: Association for Supervision and Curriculum Development.			★	★		★	★	
Dockett, S., & Perry, B. (2001). Starting school: Effective transitions. *Early Childhood Research & Practice, 3*(2). Retrieved from http://ecrp.uiuc.edu/v3n2/dockett.html					★			★
Dougherty, C., & Rutherford, J. (2009). *The NCEA core practice framework: An organizing guide to sustained school improvement*. Austin, TX: National Center for Educational Achievement.	★	★	★	★		★	★	
Dynarski, M., Clarke, L., Cobb, B., Finn, J., Rumberger, R., & Smink, J. (2008). *Dropout prevention: A practice guide* (NCEE 2008-4025). Washington, DC: National Center for Educational Evaluation and Regional Assistance, Institute of Education Sciences, U.S. Department of Education. Retrieved from http://ies.ed.gov/ncee/wwc			★		★	★		★

Resource	Standards	Curriculum	Instruction	Assessment	Resources	Professional Staff	Policy and Governance	Family and Community
Early, D. M., Maxwell, K. L., Burchinal, M., Alva, S., Bender, R. H., Bryant, D., et al. (2007). Teachers' education, classroom quality, and young children's academic skills: Results from seven studies of preschool programs. *Child Development, 78*(2), 558–580.			★			★		
Elmore, R. F. (2000). *Building a new structure for school leadership*. Washington, DC: Albert Shanker Institute.	★		★			★	★	
Epstein, J. L. (2007). Connections count: Improving family and community involvement in secondary schools. *Principal Leadership, 8*(2), 16–22.						★	★	★
Ferguson, C. (2005). *Beyond the building: A facilitation guide for school, family, and community connections*. Austin, TX: SEDL.			★			★	★	★
Ferguson, C., Jordan, C., & Baldwin, M. (2010). *Working systemically in action: Engaging family and community*. Austin, TX: SEDL. Retrieved from http://www.sedl.org/pubs/catalog/items/family126.html	★	★	★	★	★	★	★	★
Ferlazzo, L. (2011). Involvement or engagement? *Educational Leadership, 68*(8), 10–14.								★
Ferlazzo, L., & Hammond, L. A. (2009). *Building parent engagement in schools*. Santa Barbara, CA: Linworth.								★

(Continued)

Resource	Standards	Curriculum	Instruction	Assessment	Resources	Professional Staff	Policy and Governance	Family and Community
Frey, N., & Fisher, D. (2009). Using common formative assessments as a source of professional development in an urban American elementary school. *Teaching and Teacher Education, 25*(5), 674–680.	★		★	★		★		
Fryer, L., & Johnson, A. (2010, November). *A coherent approach to high school improvement: A district and school self-assessment tool.* Washington, DC: National High School Center. Retrieved from http://www.betterhighschools.org/docs/EightElementsNeedsAssessment.pdf	★	★	★	★	★	★	★	★
Fullan, M. (2010). *All systems go: The change imperative for whole system reform.* Thousand Oaks, CA: Corwin.			★			★	★	
Fullan, M. (2010). The big ideas behind whole system reform. *Education Canada, 50*(3), 24–27.						★	★	
Fullan, M., Bertani, A., & Quinn, J. (2004). New lessons for districtwide reform. *Educational Leadership, 61*(7), 42–46. Retrieved from http://www.ascd.org/publications/educational-leadership/apr04/vol61/num07/New-Lessons-for-Districtwide-Reform.aspx			★		★	★	★	★
Fullan, M., Cuttress, C., & Kilcher, A. (2005). Eight forces for leaders of change. *Journal of Staff Development, 26*(4), 54–64.				★		★		

Resource	Standards	Curriculum	Instruction	Assessment	Resources	Professional Staff	Policy and Governance	Family and Community
Garmston, R., & Wellman, B. (2009). *The adaptive school: A sourcebook for developing collaborative groups* (2nd ed.). Norwood, MA: Christopher Gordon.						★		
Gates, G., & Robinson, S. (2009). Delving into teacher collaboration: Untangling problems and solutions for leadership. *NASSP Bulletin, 93*(3), 145–165.		★	★			★	★	
Gersten, R., Baker, S. K., Shanahan, T., Linan-Thompson, S., Collins, P., & Scarcella, R. (2007). *Effective literacy and English language instruction for English learners in the elementary grades: A practice guide* (NCEE 2007-4011). Washington, DC: National Center for Education Evaluation and Regional Assistance, Institute of Education Sciences, U.S. Department of Education. Retrieved from http://ies.ed.gov/ncee/wwc/PracticeGuide.aspx?sid=6		★	★	★		★	★	

(*Continued*)

Resource	Standards	Curriculum	Instruction	Assessment	Resources	Professional Staff	Policy and Governance	Family and Community
Gersten, R., Beckmann, S., Clarke, B., Foegen, A., Marsh, L., Star, J. R., & Witzel, B. (2009). *Assisting students struggling with mathematics: Response to Intervention (RtI) for elementary and middle schools* (NCEE 2009-4060). Washington, DC: National Center for Education Evaluation and Regional Assistance, Institute of Education Sciences, U.S. Department of Education. Retrieved from http://ies.ed.gov/ncee/wwc/practiceguide.aspx?sid=2		★	★	★	★	★	★	
Gersten, R., Compton, D., Connor, C. M., Dimino, J., Santoro, L., Linan-Thompson, S., & Tilly, W. D. (2009). *Assisting students struggling with reading: Response to intervention and multi-tier intervention for reading in the primary grades. A practice guide.* (NCEE 2009-4045). Washington, DC: National Center for Education Evaluation and Regional Assistance, Institute of Education Sciences, U.S. Department of Education. http://ies.ed.gov/ncee/wwc/PracticeGuide.aspx?sid=3		★	★	★		★	★	

Resource	Standards	Curriculum	Instruction	Assessment	Resources	Professional Staff	Policy and Governance	Family and Community
Glick, J. E., & Hohmann-Marrott, B. (2007). Academic performance of young children in immigrant families: The significance of race, ethnicity, and national origins. *International Migration Review, 41*(2), 371–402.					★			★
Graczewski, C., Knudson, J., & Holtzman, D. J. (2009). Instructional leadership in practice: What does it look like, and what influence does it have? *Journal of Education for Students Placed at Risk, 14*(1), 72–96.		★	★			★		
Guarino, C., Santibañez, L., Daley, G. A., & Brewer, D. (2004). *A review of the research literature on teacher recruitment and retention* (TR-164-EDU). Santa Monica, CA: Rand Corporation. Retrieved from http://www.rand.org/pubs/technical_reports/TR164						★	★	
Halpern, D., Aronson, J., Reimer, N., Simpkins, S., Star, J., & Wentzel, K. (2007). *Encouraging girls in math and science* (NCER 2007-2003). Washington, DC: National Center for Education Research, Institute of Education Sciences, U.S. Department of Education. Retrieved from http://ies.ed.gov/ncee/wwc/PracticeGuide.aspx?sid=5			★	★		★		

(Continued)

Resource	Standards	Curriculum	Instruction	Assessment	Resources	Professional Staff	Policy and Governance	Family and Community
Hamilton, L., Halverson, R., Jackson, S., Mandinach, E., Supovitz, J., & Wayman, J. (2009). *Using student achievement data to support instructional decision making* (NCEE 2009-4067). Washington, DC: National Center for Education Evaluation and Regional Assistance, Institute of Education Sciences, U.S. Department of Education. Retrieved from http://ies.ed.gov/ncee/wwc/PracticeGuide.aspx?sid=12			★	★	★	★		
Hassel, B. C., & Hassel, E. A. (2010). *Opportunity at the top: How America's best teachers could close the gaps, raise the bar, and keep our nation great.* Chapel Hill, NC: Public Impact.			★		★	★	★	
Haynes, M. (2011, January). *Meeting the challenge: The role of school leaders in turning around the lowest-performing high schools* (Policy brief). Washington, DC: Alliance for Excellent Education.	★	★	★	★		★	★	
Heck, R. H., & Hallinger, P. (2009). Assessing the contribution of distributed leadership to school improvement and growth in math achievement. *American Educational Research Journal, 46*(3), 659–689.			★			★	★	

Resource	Standards	Curriculum	Instruction	Assessment	Resources	Professional Staff	Policy and Governance	Family and Community
Henderson, A., & Mapp, K. (2002). *A new wave of evidence: The impact of school, family, and community connections on student achievement* (Annual synthesis 2002). Austin, TX: SEDL. Retrieved from http://www.sedl.org/connections/resources/evidence.pdf					★	★	★	★
Heppen, J. B., & Therriault, S. B. (2008, July). *Developing early warning systems to identify potential high school dropouts.* Washington, DC: National High School Center.					★		★	
Herman, R., Dawson, P., Dee, T., Greene, J., Maynard, R., Redding, S., & Darwin, M. (2008). *Turning around chronically low-performing schools: A practice guide* (NCEE #2008- 4020). Washington, DC: National Center for Education Evaluation and Regional Assistance, Institute of Education Sciences, U.S. Department of Education. Retrieved from http://ies.ed.gov/ncee/wwc/PracticeGuide.aspx?sid=7			★	★		★	★	
Hill, N. E., & Tyson, D. F. (2009). Parental involvement in middle school: A meta-analytic assessment of the strategies that promote achievement. *Developmental Psychology, 45*(3), 740–763.								★

(Continued)

Resource	Standards	Curriculum	Instruction	Assessment	Resources	Professional Staff	Policy and Governance	Family and Community
Hirsch, E. (2008). *Key issue: Identifying professional contexts to support highly effective teachers.* Washington, DC: National Comprehensive Center for Teacher Quality.			★		★	★	★	★
Hirsh, S. (2010). Teacher evaluation: An opportunity to leverage learning at all levels. *The Learning System,* 6(1). (Oxford, OH: Learning Forward.)			★			★	★	
Holcomb, E. L. (2008). *Asking the right questions: Tools for collaboration and school change* (3rd ed.). Thousand Oaks, CA: Corwin.		★	★	★		★	★	★
Honig, M. I., Copland, M. A., Rainey, L., Lorton, J. A., & Newton, M. (2010). *Central office transformation for district-wide teaching and learning improvement.* Seattle: University of Washington Center for the Study of Teaching and Policy. Retrieved from http://depts.washington.edu/ctpmail/PDFs/S2-CentralAdmin-04-2010.pdf					★	★	★	★
Hord, S. M., Roussin, J. L., & Sommers, W. A. (2010). *Guiding professional learning communities: Inspiration, challenge, surprise, and meaning.* Thousand Oaks, CA: Corwin.			★	★		★		

Resource	Standards	Curriculum	Instruction	Assessment	Resources	Professional Staff	Policy and Governance	Family and Community
Hoyert, M. S., & O'Dell, C. D. (2006). A brief intervention to aid struggling students: A case of too much motivation? *Journal of Scholarship of Teaching and Learning, 6*(1), 1–13. Retrieved from https://www.iupui.edu/~josotl/toc.php?id=10			★					
Humphrey, D., Koppich, J., & Hough, H. (2005). Sharing the wealth: National board certified teachers and the students who need them most. *Education Policy Analysis Archives, 13*(18). Retrieved from http://epaa.asu.edu/epaa/v13n18						★	★	
Ingersoll, R., & Merrill, L. (2010). Who's teaching our children? *Educational Leadership, 67*(8), 14–20.					★	★	★	
Johnson, P. E., & Chrispeels, J. H. (2010). Linking the central office and its schools for reform. *Educational Administration Quarterly, 46*(5), 738–775. Retrieved from http://eaq.sagepub.com/content/46/5/738			★			★	★	
Jolly, A. (2005). *A facilitator's guide to professional learning teams.* Greensboro: School of Education, University of North Carolina at Greensboro, SERVE. Retrieved from http://www.eric.ed.gov/ERICWebPortal/recordDetail?accno=ED485208			★	★		★		

(Continued)

Resource	Standards	Curriculum	Instruction	Assessment	Resources	Professional Staff	Policy and Governance	Family and Community
Joyce, B., Showers, B., & Fullan, M. (2002). *Student achievement through staff development* (3rd ed.). Alexandria, VA: ASCD.		★	★			★	★	
Kamil, M. L., Borman, G. D., Dole, J., Kral, C. C., Salinger, T., & Torgesen, J. (2008). *Improving adolescent literacy: Effective classroom and intervention practices: A practice guide* (NCEE #2008-4027). Washington, DC: National Center for Education Evaluation and Regional Assistance, Institute of Education Sciences, U.S. Department of Education. Retrieved from http://ies.ed.gov/ncee/wwc/PracticeGuide.aspx?sid=8			★	★	★			
Kilbane, J. F., Jr. (2009). Factors in sustaining professional learning community. *NASSP Bulletin,* 9(3), 184–205.						★	★	★	
Kilgore, S. B., & Reynolds, K. J. (2010). *From silos to systems: Reframing schools for success.* Thousand Oaks, CA: Corwin.		★	★			★	★	★
Killion, J. (2010, December/January). High-impact coaching ensures maximum results. *The Learning System,* 5(4), 1, 6–7.			★	★	★	★	★	
Killion, J., & Roy, P. (2009). *Becoming a learning school.* Oxford, OH: National Staff Development Council.			★	★		★	★	

Resource	Standards	Curriculum	Instruction	Assessment	Resources	Professional Staff	Policy and Governance	Family and Community
Killion, J., & Roy, P. (2010, Spring). The changing role of central office staff. *The Learning System, 5*(5), 1, 6–7.			★	★	★	★	★	
Kim, J. J., & Crasco, L. M. (2006). Best policies and practices in urban educational reform: A summary of empirical analysis focusing on student achievement and equity. *Journal of Education for Students Placed at Risk, 11*(1), 19–37.			★			★	★	★
Knapp, M. S., Copland, M. A., Honig, M. I., Plecki, M. L., & Portin, B. S. (2010, August). *Learning-focused leadership and leadership support: Meanings and practice in urban systems.* Seattle: University of Washington Center for the Study of Teaching and Policy. Retrieved from http://www .wallacefoundation.org/Pages/ the-practice-learning-focused -leadership-support-urban -systems.aspx			★		★	★	★	
Knapp, M. S., Copland, M. A., & Talbert, J. E. (2003, February). *Leading for learning: Reflective tools for school and district leaders.* Seattle, WA: Center for the Study of Teaching and Policy. Retrieved from http://depts .washington.edu/ctpmail/ PDFs/LforLSummary-02-03 .pdf			★	★		★	★	★

(Continued)

Resource	Standards	Curriculum	Instruction	Assessment	Resources	Professional Staff	Policy and Governance	Family and Community
Kowal, J., Hassel, E. A., & Hassel, B. (2009). *Successful school turnarounds: Seven steps for district leaders.* Washington, DC: Center for Comprehensive School Reform and Improvement. Retrieved from http://www.centerforcsri.org/files/centerIssueBriefSept09.pdf			★			★	★	★
Laird, E. (2006, September). *Data use drives school and district improvement.* Washington, DC: Council of Chief State Schools Officers. Retrieved from http://www.dataqualitycampaign.org/resources/details/35				★	★		★	
LaMonte, H., & Delagardelle, M. (2009). Seeing the light. *American School Board Journal, 196*(8), 27–30.			★				★	★
Land, D. (2002, January). *Local school boards under review: Their role and effectiveness in relation to students' academic achievement.* Washington, DC: Center for Research on the Education of Students Placed at Risk.					★	★	★	
Leithwood, K., Louis, K. S., Anderson, S., & Wahlstrom, K. (2004). *How leadership influences student learning.* St. Paul: Center for Applied Research and Educational Improvement, University of Minnesota.						★	★	

Resource	Standards	Curriculum	Instruction	Assessment	Resources	Professional Staff	Policy and Governance	Family and Community
Leithwood, K., Mascall, B., Strauss, T., Sacks, R., Memon, N., & Yashkina, A. (2007). Distributing leadership to make schools smarter: Taking the ego out of the system. *Leadership and Policy in Schools, 6*(1), 37–67.						★	★	
Louis, K. S., Leithwood, K., Wahlstrom, K. L., & Anderson, S. E. (2010, July). *Learning from leadership: Investigating the links to improved student learning.* St. Paul: Center for Applied Research and Educational Improvement, University of Minnesota.	★	★	★		★	★	★	★
Marsh, J. A., Kerr, K. A., Ikemoto, G. S., Darilek, H., Suttorp, M., Zimmer, R. W., & Barney, H. (2005). *The role of districts in fostering instructional improvement.* Santa Monica, CA: RAND Corporation.			★	★		★	★	
Martin, R. A. (2006). Wake-up call brings a jolt of alignment to the curriculum. *Journal of Staff Development, 27*(1), 53–55.	★	★	★	★		★		
Marzano, R. J. (2003). *What works in schools: Translating research to action.* Alexandria, VA: Association for Supervision and Curriculum Development.	★	★	★			★	★	
Marzano, R. J. (2007). *The art and science of teaching: A comprehensive framework for effective instruction.* Alexandria, VA: ASCD.			★			★		

(Continued)

Resource	Standards	Curriculum	Instruction	Assessment	Resources	Professional Staff	Policy and Governance	Family and Community
Marzano, R. J., Frontier, T., & Haystead, M. W. (2008). *Making standards useful in the classroom.* Alexandria, VA: ASCD.	★	★	★	★				
Marzano, R. J., & Waters, T. (2009). *District leadership that works: Striking the right balance.* Bloomington, IN: Solution Tree.						★	★	
Marzano, R. J., Waters, T., & McNulty, B. A. (2005). *School leadership that works: From research to results.* Alexandria, VA: ASCD.						★	★	
McLaughlin, M., & Talbert, J. (2003). *Reforming districts: How districts support school reform* (Research Report, R-03-6). Seattle, WA: Center for the Study of Teaching and Policy. Retrieved from http://depts.washington.edu/ctpmail/PDFs/ReformingDistricts-09-2003.pdf				★	★	★	★	
Miller, M. (2009, August). *Achieving a wealth of riches: Delivering on the promise of data to transform teaching and learning* (Policy brief). Washington, DC: Alliance for Excellent Education.				★	★	★	★	

Resource	Standards	Curriculum	Instruction	Assessment	Resources	Professional Staff	Policy and Governance	Family and Community
Mizell, H. (2010). *Why professional development matters.* Oxford, OH: Learning Forward. Retrieved from http://www.learningforward.org/advancing/Why_PD_Matters_Web.pdf			★		★	★	★	
Munger, L., & von Frank, V. (2010). *Change, lead, succeed: Building capacity with school leadership teams.* Oxford, OH: NSDC.						★	★	
Murphy, J. (2007). Restructuring through learning-focused leadership. In H. J. Walberg (Ed.), *Handbook on restructuring and substantial school improvement* (pp. 71–83). Lincoln, IL: Center on Innovation and Improvement. Retrieved from www.centerii.org	★	★				★	★	★
Murphy, J., & Meyers, C. V. (2008). *Turning around failing schools: Leadership lessons from the organizational sciences.* Thousand Oaks, CA: Corwin.					★	★	★	
Nodine, T. R., & Petrides, L. A. (2006). Indicators & outcomes. *T.H.E. Journal, 33*(10), 46–48, 50–51.					★	★	★	★
O'Doherty, A., & Ovando, M. N. (2009). Drivers of success: One district's process for closing achievement gaps in a post-No Child Left Behind context. *Journal of School Leadership, 19*(1), 6–32.					★	★	★	

(Continued)

Resource	Standards	Curriculum	Instruction	Assessment	Resources	Professional Staff	Policy and Governance	Family and Community
Pashler, H., Bain, P. M., Bottge, B. A., Graesser, A., Koedinger, K., McDaniel, M., & Metcalfe, J. (2007). *Organizing instruction and study to improve student learning* (NCER 2007-2004). Washington, DC: National Center for Education Research, Institute of Education Sciences, U.S. Department of Education. Retrieved from http://ies.ed.gov/ncer/pubs/practiceguides/20072004.asp			★	★		★		
Perkins, B. K. (2007). *Where we teach: The CUBE survey of urban school climate.* Alexandria, VA: National School Boards Association.			★			★		★
Perkins, B. K. (2008). *What we think: Parental perceptions of urban school climate.* Alexandria, VA: National School Boards Association.								★
Petrides, L. A. (2006). Using data to improve instruction. *T.H.E. Journal, 33*(9), 32–34, 36–37.				★	★	★		★
Pinkus, L. (2008, August). *Using early-warning data to improve graduation rates: Closing cracks in the education system* (Policy brief). New York, NY: Alliance for Excellent Education.				★	★	★		
Pitler, H. (2009, December/January). Classroom walk-throughs. *The Learning Principal, 4*(4), 1, 6–7.			★		★	★	★	

Resource	*Standards*	*Curriculum*	*Instruction*	*Assessment*	*Resources*	*Professional Staff*	*Policy and Governance*	*Family and Community*
Plecki, M. L., Knapp, M. S., Castaneda, T., Halverson, T., SaSota, R., & Lochmiller, C. (2009, October). *How leaders invest staffing resources for learning improvement*. Seattle: University of Washington Center for the Study of Teaching and Policy. Retrieved from www.ctpweb.org					★	★	★	
Portin, B. S., Knapp, M. S., Dareff, S., Feldman, S., Russell, F. A., Samuelson, C., & Yeh, T. L. (2009, October). *Leadership for learning improvement in urban schools*. Seattle: University of Washington Center for the Study of Teaching and Policy. Retrieved from www.ctpweb.org		★	★	★		★	★	
Quint, J., Thompson, S. L., & Bald, M. (2008, October). *Relationships, rigor, and readiness: Strategies for improving high schools*. New York, NY: MDRC.	★	★	★		★	★	★	★
Redding, S. (2007). Systems for improved teaching and learning. In H. J. Walberg (Ed.), *Handbook on restructuring and substantial school improvement* (pp. 99–112). Lincoln, IL: Center on Innovation and Improvement. Retrieved from www.centerii.org	★	★	★	★		★	★	★

(Continued)

Resource	Standards	Curriculum	Instruction	Assessment	Resources	Professional Staff	Policy and Governance	Family and Community
Rhim, L. M., Kowal, J. M., Hassell, B. C., & Hassel, E. A. (2007). *School turnarounds: A review of the cross-sector evidence on dramatic organizational improvement.* Lincoln, IL: Center on Innovation & Improvement. Retrieved from http://www .centerii.org			★			★	★	★
Rorrer, A. K., Skrla, L., & Scheurich, J. J. (2008). Districts as institutional actors in educational reform. *Educational Administration Quarterly, 44*(3), 307–358.						★	★	
Roy, P., & Hord, S. M. (2003). *Moving NSDC's staff development standards into practice: Innovation configurations.* Oxford, OH: NSDC.						★	★	
Rumberger, R., & Lim, S. A. (2008, October). *Why students drop out of school: A review of 25 years of research.* (California Dropout Research Project, Policy Brief 15). Retrieved from http://www.cdrp.ucsb.edu/ pubs_reports.htm					★		★	
Sanders, M. G. (2008). How parent liaisons can help bridge the home-school gap. *Journal of Educational Research, 101*(5), 287–297.						★		★

Resource	Standards	Curriculum	Instruction	Assessment	Resources	Professional Staff	Policy and Governance	Family and Community
Sanders, N. M., & Kearney, K. M. (Eds.). (2008). *Performance expectations and indicators for education leaders.* Washington, DC: Council of Chief State School Officers, State Consortium of Educational Leadership. Retrieved from http://www.ccsso.org/ Documents/2008/ Peformance_Indicators_ 2008.pdf	★	★	★	★	★	★	★	★
Sashkin, M., & Egermeier, J. (1993). *School change models and processes: A review and synthesis of research and practice.* Washington, DC: U.S. Government Printing Office (ERIC Document Reproduction Service No. 351 757).								
Schmoker, M. (2006). *Results now: How we can achieve unprecedented improvement in teaching and learning.* Alexandria, VA: ASCD.		★	★		★	★	★	
Senge, P., Cambron-McCabe, N., Lucas, T., Smith, B., Dutton, J., & Kleiner, A. (2000). *Schools that learn.* New York, NY: Doubleday.			★			★	★	★

(*Continued*)

Resource	Standards	Curriculum	Instruction	Assessment	Resources	Professional Staff	Policy and Governance	Family and Community
Shanahan, T., Callison, K., Carriere, C., Duke, N. K., Pearson, P. D., Schatschneider, C., & Torgesen, J. (2010, September). *Improving reading comprehension in kindergarten through 3rd grade: A practice guide* (NCEE 2010-4038). Washington, DC: National Center for Education Evaluation and Regional Assistance, Institute of Education Sciences, U.S. Department of Education. Retrieved from http://ies.ed.gov/ncee/wwc/PracticeGuide.aspx?sid=14			★			★		
Sheldon, S. (2007). Improving student attendance with school, family, and community partnerships. *Journal of Education Research, 100*(5), 267–275.							★	★
Southwest Comprehensive Center at WestEd. (2008). *A guide for comprehensive needs assessment.* Retrieved from http://www.cde.state.co.us/FedPrograms/dl/consapp_na_guide.pdf		★	★	★	★	★	★	★
Sparks, D. (2004). Focusing staff development on improving the learning for all students. In G. Cawelti (Ed.), *Handbook of research on improving student achievement* (3rd ed., pp. 245–255). Arlington, VA: Educational Research Service.			★		★	★	★	

Resource	Standards	Curriculum	Instruction	Assessment	Resources	Professional Staff	Policy and Governance	Family and Community
Spillane, J. P., & Diamond, J. B. (2007). *Distributed leadership in practice.* New York, NY: Teachers College Press.						★	★	
St. George, C. Y. (2010). How can elementary teachers collaborate more effectively with parents to support student literacy learning? *Delta Kappa Gamma Bulletin, 76*(2), 32–38.			★			★		★
Steele, J. L., & Boudett, K. P. (2008, December / 2009, January). The collaborative advantage. *Educational Leadership, 66*(4), 54–59.			★	★		★		
Thornton, B., Peltier, G., & Perreault, G. (2004). Systems thinking: A skill to improve student thinking. *The Clearing House, 77*(5), 222–227.								
Thornton, B., Shepperson, T., & Canavero, S. (2007). A systems approach to school improvement: Program evaluation and organizational learning. *Education, 128*(1), 48–55.						★		
Togneri, W., & Anderson, S. E. (2003). *Beyond islands of excellence: What districts can do to improve instruction and achievement in all schools—A leadership brief.* Washington, DC: Learning First Alliance. Retrieved from www .learningfirst.org/sites/default/ files/assets/biefullreport.pdf			★	★		★	★	

(Continued)

Resource	Standards	Curriculum	Instruction	Assessment	Resources	Professional Staff	Policy and Governance	Family and Community
Tschannen-Moran, M. (2004). *Trust matters: Leadership for successful schools.* San Francisco, CA: Jossey-Bass.			★			★		
Tucci, T. N. (2009). *Whole school reform: Transforming the nation's low-performing high schools.* Washington, DC: Alliance for Excellent Education.		★	★		★	★	★	
Von Frank, V. (2008). *Creating a culture of professional learning.* Oxford, OH: NSDC			★			★		
Von Frank, V. (2009). District pulls together in pursuit of excellence. *The Learning System, 4*(7), 1, 4–7. Oxford, OH: NSDC						★	★	
Von Frank, V. (2010). Trust matters—for educators, parents, and students. *Tools for Schools, 14*(1). Oxford, OH: Learning Forward.						★		★
Von Frank, V. (2011). Interactions shape distributed leadership. *The Learning Principal, 6*(2), 1, 4–5.						★	★	
Wahlstrom, K., & Louis, K. S. (2008). How teachers experience principal leadership. *Educational Administration Quarterly, 44*(4), 458–495.			★			★	★	

Resource	Standards	Curriculum	Instruction	Assessment	Resources	Professional Staff	Policy and Governance	Family and Community
Walberg, H. J. (2007). Changing and monitoring instruction. In H. J. Walberg (Ed.), *Handbook on restructuring and substantial school improvement* (pp. 85–98). Lincoln, IL: Center on Innovation and Improvement. Retrieved from www.centerii .org	★		★	★	★	★		★
Walberg, H. J. (2010). *Improving student learning: Action principles for families, classrooms, schools, districts, and states.* Lincoln, IL: Center on Innovation and Improvement. Retrieved from http://www .centerii.org/	★	★	★	★	★	★	★	★
Walker, J. (2009). Reorganizing leaders' time: Does it create better schools for students? *NASSP Bulletin, 93*(4), 213–226.						★	★	
Wallace Foundation Staff. (2011). *Research findings to support effective educational policies: A guide for policymakers* (2nd ed.). New York, NY: Wallace Foundation. Retrieved from http://www .wallacefoundation .org/Home%20Page%20 Feature/Findings-to-Support -Effective-Educational-Policy -Making.pdf					★	★	★	★

(Continued)

Resource	Standards	Curriculum	Instruction	Assessment	Resources	Professional Staff	Policy and Governance	Family and Community
Wallach, C. A., Lambert, M. B., Copland, M., & Lowry, L. K. (2005, Autumn). *Distributing leadership: Moving from high school hierarchy to shared responsibility*. Seattle, WA: Bill & Melinda Gates Foundation, Small Schools Project. Retrieved from http://www.abeoschoolchange.org/wp-content/uploads/2011/02/distributing-leadership.pdf						★	★	
Wellman, B., & Lipton, L. (2003). *Data-driven dialogue: A facilitator's guide to collaborative inquiry*. Sherman, CT: MiraVia.						★		
Wheelan, S. A. (2005). *Faculty groups: From frustration to collaboration*. Thousand Oaks, CA: Corwin.			★	★		★		
Wolff, L. A., McClelland, S. S., & Stewart, S. E. (2010). The relationship between adequate yearly progress and the quality of professional development. *Journal of School Leadership, 20*(3), 304–322.			★	★		★		★

Resource	Standards	Curriculum	Instruction	Assessment	Resources	Professional Staff	Policy and Governance	Family and Community
Yoon, K. S., Duncan, T., Lee, S.-W., Scarloss, B., & Shapley, K. L. (2007). *Reviewing the evidence on how teacher professional development affects student achievement* (Issues & Answers Report, REL 2007-No. 033). Washington, DC: U.S. Department of Education, Institute of Education Sciences, National Center for Educational Evaluation and Regional Assistance, Regional Educational Laboratory Southwest. Retrieved from http://ies.ed.gov/ncee/edlabs/regions/southwest/pdf/REL_2007033_sum.pdf			★			★		
Ziegler, C. (2006). Walk-throughs provide stepped-up support. *Journal of Staff Development, 27*(4), 53–56.			★			★		

In addition to the resources listed in the bibliography, the following websites offer useful guidance and documents for districts and schools implementing a systemic improvement approach.

- U.S. Department of Education
  http://www.ed.gov
- Doing What Works
  http://dww.ed.gov/
- National Center for Education Research
  http://ies.ed.gov/ncer/
- Regional Education Laboratories
  http://ies.ed.gov/ncee/edlabs/
- What Works Clearinghouse
  http://ies.ed.gov/ncee/wwc/
- Education Resources Information Center (ERIC)
  http://eric.ed.gov/

- National Comprehensive Content Centers
  Assessment and Accountability Content Center
  http://www.aacompcenter.org
- National High School Center
  http://www.betterhighschools.org
- Center on Innovation and Improvement
  http://www.centerii.org
- Center on Instruction
  http://www.centeroninstruction.org
- National Comprehensive Center for Teacher Quality
  http://www.tqsource.org

 An electronic version of the Bibliography Matrix and a list of websites is available in the Research Module found on the companion website.

References

Bernhardt, V. L. (2009). *Data, data, everywhere: Bringing all the data together for continuous school improvement*. Larchmont, NY: Eye on Education.

Blum, R., & Landis, S. (1998). *Scaling up continuous improvement: A case description of Onward to Excellence in Mississippi*. Portland, OR: Northwest Regional Educational Laboratory.

Bossert, S. (1985, May). Effective elementary schools. In R. Kyle (Ed.), *Reaching for excellence: An effective schools sourcebook* (pp. 39–53). Washington, DC: U.S. Government Printing Office.

Bryk, A. S., & Schneider, B. L. (2002). *Trust in schools: A core resource for improvement*. New York, NY: Russell Sage Foundation.

Bryk, A. S., Sebring, P. B., Allensworth, E., Luppescu, S., & Easton, J. Q. (2010). *Organizing schools for improvement: Lessons from Chicago*. Chicago, IL: University Of Chicago Press.

Chenowith, K. (2007). *"It's being done": Academic success in unexpected schools*. Cambridge, MA: Harvard Education Press.

Cohen, M., & Ginsburg, A. (2001, January). *School improvement report: Executive order on actions for turning around low-performing schools*. Washington, DC: U.S. Department of Education.

Corallo, C., & McDonald, D. H. (2002, January). *What works with low-performing schools: A review of research*. Charleston, WV: AEL.

Cowan, D. F. (2006). Creating learning communities in low-performing sites: A systemic approach to alignment. *Journal of School Leadership, 16*(5), 596–610.

Cowan, D. (2009, November). Creating a community of professional learners: An inside view. *SEDL Letter, 21*(1), 20–25.

Cowan, D. F., Joyner, S., & Beckwith, S. (2008). *Working systemically in action: A guide for facilitators*. Austin, TX: SEDL.

Edmonds, R. (1979). Effective schools for the urban poor. *Educational Leadership, 37*(1), 15–23.

Gideon, B. H. (2002). Supporting a collaborative culture. *Principal Leadership, 3*(1), 41–44.

Hallinger, P., & Murphy, J. (1986). The social context of effective schools. *American Journal of Education, 94*(3), 328–355.

Herman, P., Dawson, P., Dee, T., Greene, J., Maynard, R., Redding, S., & Darwin, M. (2008). *Turning around chronically low-performing schools: A practice guide* (NCEE #2008–4020). Washington, DC: National Center for Education Evaluation and Regional Assistance, Institute of Education Sciences, U.S. Department of

Education. Retrieved September 15, 2008, from http://ies.ed.gov/ncee/wwc/practiceguides

Holcomb, E. L. (2008). *Asking the right questions: Tools for collaboration and school change (3rd. ed.)*. Thousand Oaks, CA: Corwin.

Huie, S. B., Buttram, J. L., Deviney, F. P., Murphy, K. M., & Ramos, M. A. (2004). *Alignment in SEDL's Working Systemically model* (Research report). Austin, TX: SEDL.

Jenlink, P. M., Reigeluth, C. M., Carr, A. A., & Nelson, L. M. (1998). Guidelines for facilitating systemic change in school districts. *Systems Research and Behavioral Science, 15*(3), 217–233.

Lezotte, L. W., & Jacoby, B. C. (1992). *Sustainable school reform: The district context for school improvement.* Okemos, MI: Effective Schools Products.

Mid-continent Research for Education and Learning. (2003). *Sustaining school improvement* (Leadership Folio Series). Aurora, CO: Author.

Murphy, J., & Meyers, C. V. (2008). *Turning around failing schools.* Thousand Oaks, CA: Corwin.

Newmann, F. M., Smith, B., Allensworth, E., & Bryk, A. S. (2001, Winter). Instructional program coherence: What it is and why it should guide school improvement policy. *Educational Evaluation and Policy Analysis, 23*(4), 213–227.

Rorrer, A. K., Skrla, L., & Scheurich, J. J. (2008). Districts as institutional actors in educational reform. *Educational Administration Quarterly, 44*(3), 307–358.

Sashkin, M., & Egermeier, J. (1993). *School change models and processes: A review and synthesis of research and practice.* Washington, DC: U.S. Department of Education.

Schmoker, M. (2011). First things first: What we teach, how we teach—and literacy. In M. Schmoker, *Focus: Elevating the essentials to radically improve student learning* (pp. 9–89). Alexandria, VA: Association for Supervision and Curriculum Development.

Senge, P., Cambron-McCabe, N., Lucas, T., Smith, B., Dutton, J., & Kleiner, A. (2000). *Schools that learn.* New York, NY: Doubleday.

Southwest Educational Development Laboratory (SEDL). (2000). *Creating knowledge to build high-performing learning communities: A proposal to serve as the regional educational laboratory for the southwestern region.* Austin, TX: Author.

Sparks, D. (2004). Focusing staff development on improving the learning for all students. In G. Cawelti (Ed.), *Handbook of research on improving student achievement* (3rd ed., pp. 245–255). Arlington, VA: Educational Research Service.

Sparks, D., & Hirsh, S. (1997). *A new vision for staff development.* Oxford, OH: National Staff Development Council.

Stringfield, S. (1995). Attempts to enhance students' learning: A search for valid programs and highly reliable implementation techniques. *School Effectiveness and School Improvement, 6*(1), 67–96.

Teddlie, C., & Stringfield, S. (1993). *School matters: Lessons learned from a 10-year study of school effects.* New York, NY: Teachers College Press.

Thornton, B., Shepperson, T., & Canavero, S. (2007). A systems approach to school improvement: Program evaluation and organizational learning. *Education, 128*(1), 48–55.

Wellman, B., & Lipton, L. (2004). *Data driven dialogue: A facilitator's guide to collaborative inquiry.* Sherman, CT: MiraVia, LLC.

Index

Pages followed by f or t indicate figures or tables

CORWIN
A SAGE Company

The Corwin logo—a raven striding across an open book—represents the union of courage and learning. Corwin is committed to improving education for all learners by publishing books and other professional development resources for those serving the field of PreK–12 education. By providing practical, hands-on materials, Corwin continues to carry out the promise of its motto: **"Helping Educators Do Their Work Better."**